North on 101

A MEMOIR

Anne Starr

What struck me over and over again, as I read Anne Starr's memoir, is how much life there is contained in these absorbing pages. And no one is more alive than Mansfield who, even in his last days, keeps saying YES! *North on 101* is a beautiful and compelling account of Mansfield's life as a brother and an artist, and of the devoted sister who responds to his summons.

—**Margot Livesey**
THE ROAD FROM BELHAVEN
and THE BOY IN THE FIELD

A profound journey through a beloved brother's illness and death, told by a brilliant writer. I have never read such an acutely rendered and loving portrait, or such a generous and astute reckoning with love and loss. Starr's language is pitch-perfect and gorgeous. I will not forget these people, or this profoundly beautiful book.

—**Meredith Hall**
BENEFICENCE and WITHOUT A MAP

A sister's poignant memoir of an older brother: their childhood together, his move to sixties San Francisco—then, suddenly, a mid-life call to help him to navigate the ravages of cancer. An impressive account of life—and death.

—**Eileen Christelow**
FIVE LITTLE MONKEYS series

Anne Starr reveals the history that set her in motion to care for her beloved brother Mansfield as he is ravaged by cancer. With intricacy and passion, she describes the infinite doors that open and close in life, until the path narrows and leaves only one more opening, and then, *the* close. Anne's lionhearted prose broke my heart: her writing is vivid, tenacious and an expression of our greatest emotion—love.

—**Cliff Hakim**
WALK IN MY SHOES, THE PATH
TO EMPATHY AND COMPASSION

Anne Starr offers a nuanced and poignant portrait of her beloved brother from the vantage point of caring for him during last days. In so doing she reveals herself to be as brilliant and complex a character as her intriguing brother.

—**Grady McGonagill**

With growing and pained self-awareness, Anne Starr chronicles the life, cancer diagnosis, and death of her beloved brother. Too often we turn away from death, but Starr turns toward the light. North on 101 is a beautiful, devastating, and heart-wrenching treatise on faith: in family, in friends, in life, in death.

—**Catherine Parnell**
THE KINGDOM OF HIS WILL

Anne Starr has written a small, beautiful, heart-breaking memoir about her older brother, Mansfield, who came of age in the early San Francisco counterculture. Shared memories serve as counterpoint to Mansfield's vivid family of choice, who rally again and again to his support with love, grace and humor. We join them in this universal journey, told through the unique voice of her "infinitely calibrated self-consciousness."

—**William R. Torbert**
THE SECRET OF TIMELY

A compelling evocation of the living-dying "in between" Anne Starr shared with her terminally ill brother, *North 101* deploys the intense present of this intermediary space into a concentrate of unflinching self-observations, rich portrayals and moving memory gems. "A world goes inside out"—indeed, and this exquisitely crafted world gifts us with the poignant complexities and delicate complicities of a sister-brother bond.

—**Monique Pommier, Ph.D.**
HARMONY, THE HEARTBEAT OF CREATION

Paradoxically life-affirming, Anne Starr's memoir about caring for her slowly dying brother in the final months of his life is beautifully and sensitively written. She shares her own sense of inadequacy in the face of his imminent death as well as painting a colorful portrait of a man who had always been bursting with life. I came away from it touched by poignancy of witnessing the end of a life, especially a life lived so energetically and joyfully.

—**Lawrence Kessenich**
THE FURTHER ADVENTURES OF DAISY MILLER

Anne Starr has been a friend and trusted partner for many decades. So, it does not surprise me that she can be a trustworthy guide on such an intimate journey, one that we are all on, whether we recognize it or not.

—**Peter Senge**
THE FIFTH DISCIPLINE
and PRESENCE

Anne Starr's love and admiration for her brother and the intensity of her desire to understand herself are palpable in her persistent questioning and analyzing of not just the situation at hand, but also as she investigates the rich bank of memories that surface as a result of the intimacy the situation demands.

—**Mary Bonina**
MY FATHER'S EYES: A MEMOIR

North on 101 is a heart-warming testament to a sister's love for her brother as he is dying of cancer. Anne Starr does not shy away from the countless challenges and moments of doubt that arise on this journey. She is a beautiful writer, and her insights and candor will serve all of us experiencing suffering and loss.

—**Susanne Cook-Greuter**

A compelling and powerful tribute to a life. A tribute to the steadfast love of a sister for a brother. *North on 101* will leave the reader with gratitude that such love exists and can soften the passing of a soul. Deeply moving.

—**Christine Breen**
HER NAME IS ROSE

Author's Note

To protect privacy, some names are changed.

FIRST EDITION, September 2025
LIBRARY OF CONGRESS CONTROL NUMBER: *pending*
ISBN 978-1-965784-40-2 HARDBACK
ISBN 978-1-965784-20-4 PAPERBACK

Cover Graphic Design & Book Typography by Kurt Lovelace.
Cover photography by Pierian Springs Press
Cover type *Bauhaus Dessau* Alfarn by Céline Hurka,
Elia Preuss, Flavia Zimbardi,
Hidetaka Yamasaki, and Luca Pellegrini.
Chapter titles in **Jenson** by Robert Slimbach.
Chapter titles in **Baskerville**; Body text set in **Nimbus**.
Chapter dropcaps set in **Mrs Eaves XL**
by Emigre Foundry designer Zuzana Licko.
Flourishes set in Emigre Foundry **Dalliance** by Frank Heine.
Emigre Foundry **ZeitGuys** by Bob Aufuldish, Eric Donelan.
Typefaces licensed Adobe, Linotype, Emigre, & URW GmbH.

PSPRESS.PUB
PIERIAN SPRINGS PRESS, INC
30 N GOULD ST, STE 25398
SHERIDAN, WYOMING 82801-6317

For Emma and Elyse

CONTENTS

North
on
101

JOURNAL

I Am Summoned

December 2000

Mansfield's voice makes me go still. I realize I am about to step forward on a path I cannot bear to take. It is the end of 2000, the world has not fallen apart as predicted. But my equilibrium is slipping away. I listen the way an animal in danger goes quiet to scan his environment. Everything recedes, even the fresh pang of my father's recent death is set aside. I am listening to the disintegration of my own life.

My brother is matter-of-fact on the other end of the line.

"The tests show cancers throughout the belly now," he says. "Likely dozens…a whole matrix of cancers in and out of the intestines."

His mind plays lightly between fact and reflection. "There's a way to die with grace," he says "…to be delighted, like setting foot in a new country." A moment of wonder enters his voice, like sunshine coming from this picture he has just drawn.

Then, "The pain is incredible; my stomach bloats and tightens like a balloon. Treatment is no longer recommended." He pauses. "My days are numbered," he says, his voice weary, like it's an old fact no longer interesting.

His voice goes on filling the line between us, sparing me having to respond, telling me he knows there no longer is a response. His beloved daughter, Emma, who is home from college on vacation, will be going back to school in a few days. Another meeting is scheduled with Dr. Pond in a few weeks. Then he asks if I will come take him to this appointment. I am jostled from my listening.

"Yes, of course," I say. That I am in Boston, 3000 miles from where he lives outside of San Francisco, doesn't register. His West Coast family of friends is all around him there, and any one of them would have been happy to drive him the few miles from Mill Valley to San Rafael. But he is asking me. I know this is a summoning. I know to say yes, as though sealing an agreement we have from before time that is now coming due. I tell him I will be there.

When I get off the phone, I hold tight to this one thing I can do. I rearrange my schedule. I book flights. I prepare for being away. But there is another deeper rhythm at work. I want to balk and run. If I could just do that maybe this would not have to be happening. My reluctance lies low in my belly, registering as a constricting weight. Mostly I keep it in abeyance, but it catches me unawares, a momentary dread, or a pang of sorrow so deep it is as if the ground falls out from beneath me.

Lost

February 3, 2001

Driving north into San Francisco from the airport, I experience an uncertainty that escalates with each new unfamiliar crossroad. I am pulled forward in the flow of traffic, anxiety mounting to panic, until I finally declare myself lost. My mind tells me this is impossible, since it is essentially a straight road—but I admit defeat and allow myself to call my friend, Marie, to come get me. I wait outside a bookstore just off the highway. As the clamor of my agitation starts to recede, I recognize I do not want to move forward into this reality. There is no question that I will, but my mind will not accommodate it. It cannot stretch itself wide enough to contain this truth, in the way the "I" that is conceiving it cannot fathom its own demise. In this perfect bind my old phobia of taking the wheel has reasserted itself. In my early 20s this manifested as a fear of driving on fast complicated highways; later it surfaced as a kind of absence or passivity where I might have taken charge of my life. Both have converged so that now I am just grateful to sit quietly, letting the warmth of the sun wash through me. Grateful for my tolerant friend who will be here soon, and who I can follow the few miles through San Francisco's serenely grid-like streets to her house, like a docile child.

My History With Death

Death had always riveted my attention, but then I always had to look away, my fear so paralyzing it was unendurable. I tried to deny it, put it off, somehow mitigate it, cover it over to be visited later, on another day. When I was six, my pet toad George surprised us by coming home weeks after I'd dutifully returned him to his rightful pond across the way. I was so delighted when he plopped over the threshold of our dining room door in that long summer Michigan twilight that my mother agreed I could make a little nest of greens and water to keep him in. When I ran to greet him expectantly the next morning, I found him shriveled, darkened and still, with a large wasp on his back. I wailed in shock and protest, summoning my mother, who had to come and clean it up.

Our first summer in Norwich, Vermont when I was eight, I was allowed to keep some gelatinous frog eggs in water. I watched as their tails formed and they became swimmers, then their hind legs sprouted and finally their arms. I placed a fresh frog on the kitchen table to watch his first hops. When I saw he was too close to the edge, I put my arm down to form a barrier against his going over and sailing to the floor. But I miscalculated. My arm came down just below his head, partially severing his neck, the throat ballooning out horribly in a white sac that should have remained inside. I was aghast, quickly placing him in a tall pitcher of water, only to watch him sink slowly, impassively to the bottom. Though I willed him to miraculously mend, it did not happen. The small consolation I told myself was that his death was instantaneous.

When I was nine, I was entertaining myself on a lazy Saturday morning by hopping across an open stairwell to the second floor—something I was forbidden to do so as not to risk falling. The phone rang and I knew in that instant, before it was answered, that my great grand-mother had died.

When I was ten, I announced to my grandfather that he was going to live forever and need not think about having to move to a place he and my grandmother could be cared for. The knowing look he gave my mother in that moment warned of the danger and irresponsibility of my glib refusal. Later, I regularly practiced contemplating my own death.

At thirteen, in the rush of early hormones, I would be up unable to sleep well into the night, painstakingly pushing a pin into my pillowcase, spelling out words that approximated my private anguish at my inability to accommodate the fact of my eventual death. These would be words like decompose, shrivel, still, eternity, depending on my mood or what I was reading. I approached the idea again and again in my ruminating mind. Each time, though, I found I could get only so far before I blanched, my heart pounding, and had to stop. I would finally tire and fall asleep, the world no wiser as the pillowcase revealed nothing.

Early one Sunday morning when I was eighteen, during my first year of living in Boston, a policeman knocked on my door and asked if I knew a certain woman. I said yes; my apartment was above her antique store, so I saw her regularly. A body had been found, they suspected who it was and wanted to know if I could identify her. In my surprise, it didn't occur to me I could say no, so I was taken to a city morgue, right there on Berkeley Street in the middle of town. I made myself look. Standing in that small basement room on the sloping cement floor with the drain at its center, in the acrid slightly sweet smell of industrial cleaning chemicals, I studied the bloated, crumpled-in face. I noted how odd it was that a grown woman's body, in its tight grimace of death, should seem small as a child's. I nodded. The policeman said, "Are you sure?" I forced myself to look again, making certain it was indeed her graceful bone structure under that death mask. That experience was stamped into me, the shock of it returning instantly whenever I happened to smell the particular cleaning chemical used in that morgue. But I remember with shame turning away days later from her stricken mother when she came at me at a small memorial service, a stranger with a messy grief I did not know how to respond to. And the mirror experience, twenty-seven years later, when I saw my Aunt Dory standing in a hallway from such an angle that she was the perfect image of my mother, who had died just months before. I was overcome with an urge to throw my arms around her, as I never could have hugged my mother when she was alive, as if I could express in that one gesture the whole complexity of my feelings for what I had lost. But she turned away, and I was left to swallow the impulse and turn aside.

Later in that same first year in Boston, Russell, a pathologist friend, asked me if I wanted to witness an autopsy. Being eager for new life experiences, I said yes. I was entirely unprepared for the dull gray skin, the yawning chest and abdomen and the overwhelming stench of death. I had such an intense visceral reaction I had to walk out of the room and try to recover myself on the other side of the door, taking calm, deep draughts of untainted air.

It was surprisingly easy to persist in this uneasy stance toward death. The culture colluded in it. Maybe this came of being born in 1950, when our very existence was part of the collective turning away from the death of World War II. A silent deflecting might have been the only acceptable response to the long deprivation of the Depression, and then the war. Maybe it was the fact of medical advances that promised a miraculous reprieve, as though death itself could be turned away. Or at least those afflicted could be whisked away from our view, attended to amidst white gleaming surfaces and the vibrant hum of an institution. Maybe it was the new prosperity that knew no bounds and would carry us all to a transcendent future, deliver us from ordinary ends.

When Mansfield called that December evening, I could no longer look away from death. He was a life ally. Two years older than I, Mansfield had always been there. The resonances we had went back forever. Huddled under the piano in the long Michigan dusk, hearing over and over again the tortured and beautiful Rakhmaninov our mother practiced. Descending into the forbidden flooded River Rouge in Birmingham, Michigan, him tugging my hand when it was too deep and my head went under. Our awe when we learned from our grandfather that Ralph, their close friend, had a gun in his socks drawer and then actually seeing it. The particular way the light fell on the bone-white Congregational Church amidst the turning maples on a late Vermont afternoon. Our shocked recognition when we discovered, as adults, that we each carried images of our mother coming after us with a knife, though we both knew this had never occurred.

Mansfield went ahead of me. He got to do things first and then would playfully taunt me to see if I could join him. He had his picture in Vermont Life Magazine at 13 years old, later introduced me to Bob Dylan, then, what did I think of Rahsaan Roland Kirk, and hadn't I read Rushdie yet? Always we compared notes. It was unthinkable that he would not be there, that he would leave me behind.

I am a stranger

February 5, 2001

I call Mansfield from my friend's house to let him know I am on my way. I find the key where he said it would be, under a wooden toy beneath the purple potted flowers. Even in the thicket of my anxiety I feel a faint pang of delight at seeing flowers, outside, in February. When I push open the door, I find a large mattress piled high with pillows in the middle of the living room floor, and him a barely discernible mound beneath a comforter in their midst. I tiptoe to his side, crouch over, touch his shoulder and call his name. He struggles to come to, turns and lies for a moment, staring at the ceiling. He blinks up at me.

"Are you the nurse?" he asks. I say, "No, it's me. Anne. Your sister." I tell him I had spoken to him only 30 minutes before. There is no recognition. He rouses himself, sitting to rest for a moment on the edge of the mattress, then pushes himself up. He weaves his way down the short hall—touching both walls alternately to steady himself—and turns into his old bedroom. A calendar lies open on his desk, filled with his blocky architectural writing. We stand over it.

"Tell me what day it is," he says.

"It's February 5th," I say. He runs his finger over the days.

"Anne's coming at 11:00," he says, pointing at my name.

"OK," I say.

"I have to lie down now," he announces and turns and makes his way back down the hall to his bed. He crouches, slides under the comforter, and covers himself until only the top of his head shows, and then he is gone. I stand alone in the middle of the room. A pale light filters through the curtains. There is the soft sound of his breathing, and stillness. I feel empty handed, my body groping to find a signal for what to do. Then I turn, walk out the door, down the stairs and around the corner. I get into the car where my generous friend waits, pull the door closed and break into loud convulsive sobbing, the dam finally broken.

"He didn't recognize me," is all I can say to sum up my fear and anguish at his frailty and the sense of being lost in this impossible present. I lean my head against the window and look out at the clump of eucalyptus, their unfamiliar ragged bark and thin leaves.

"His friend Fran will be here soon," I say, mooring myself to the next thing as a way to move forward.

I see my place

February 6, 2001

We hold a meeting convened by the hospice nurse, Margaret, who declares Mansfield too weak to go to the doctor's appointment for which I had been summoned. He still regards me warily, as though there is some familiarity, but he can't quite place me, despite my brief second meeting with him, when Fran arrived. His politeness makes me feel a stranger to myself. But he is up sitting on one of the rolling office chairs as if holding court. I can see his friends' attention delights him, like an elixir that brings him alive. Fran chides him about getting into accidents and worrying everybody. She points out Exhibit A, the dark bruise that still shows on his forehead where he fell and hit his head while over-medicated. Mansfield looks sheepish. Elyse, his partner of many years, who still lives in Noe Valley so that Mansfield can maintain his cherished independence, describes the difficulty of scheduling a reliable stream of people to look in on him, given work schedules, distance from the city, and conflicts that invariably arise at the last minute. Her lilting southern voice makes the litany sound easy, but she has carried the burden and worry of it for a long time. Margaret finally speaks. She says a regimen can be constructed that would manage the nausea, manage the pain, and promote equilibrium and comfort. But it has to be adhered to throughout the day and night to be effective. Skipping doses then drinking from the bottle rather than meting out the pre-scribed milligrams leads to chaos: the hallucinations Mansfield insists are grand mal seizures, forgotten pots dry burning on the stove, loss of coordination and the danger of hurting himself, the inability to reliably do something as simple as insert a key into the door or make a telephone call.

I feel my attention recede from the conversation. It rises up and hovers just above me, as though I can see the whole gathering from above, as though I am both in it and outside it. Though it never occurred to me before, I see that I will live there and take care of my brother. It is like something just waiting to happen. I see it merely as a matter of having reality find its way into alignment with this knowing. At some level it has already done so. It is the simple and necessary answer that comes with no thought before the question is posed. I have no idea how I will accomplish it, but, uncharacteristically, I know that that doesn't matter at all. I announce that I will come live there, and I immediately feel the shape of the room change—the first falling into place. While this represents a seismic change for me, the conversation moves on matter-of-factly to the immediate issue of needing to get Mansfield onto a regular regimen.

The next day, I take the flight home to Boston still with this sense of directing myself from above, where everything is already clear and certain. I pay scrupulous attention to what is right in front of me moment by moment. I say what I want again and again and have the sensation of holding a space open to any possibility of fulfilling it, like a fisherman casting a wide net and trusting there will be a catch. I know the right thing is just ahead and will come and that I will recognize it even if it surprises me. There is a feeling of urgent imperative and of absolute calm. And the sense I am working on this effortlessly in every conversation, every action, even as I go about my routine day, even as I sleep.

Reports from Raymond

Early February, 2001

Elyse and I met with Raymond, Mansfield's new home health care provider, the day I flew out of San Francisco to return to Boston. Over the 10 days it took me to get ready to move to San Francisco, I received regular reports from Raymond. I loved getting these as they assuaged my concern about Mansfield being well cared for. They were filled with detail, admonitions, and sweeping generalizations. They were also windows into what I could expect. I didn't know if he was unique among home health care providers, but Raymond's reports were as exacting as one might expect to see from an investigative researcher. He wrote:

February 7

8:30 We tried to fix breakfast. Due to the strong medication of the anti-emetic cocktail, which he drank straight from the bottle according to him, he seems confused. He forgets which oven grill is on...he forgets where to put the pans...that is why kitchen control by the Care-giver is very important to avoid possible fire hazards.

12:30 I prepared lunch. He ate 3 small cuts of roasted chicken, ½ cup of peas, and a cup of yogurt. We talked a lot about philosophy, religion, Buddhism...he is a very deep thinker and he seems very profound.

2:30 I gave him the anti-emetic cocktail in 2.5 ml syringe! Never again should he drink this cocktail medicine straight from the bottle.

SUGGESTIONS AND COMMENTS: Over medication of the anti-emetic cocktail is dangerous. His use of the kitchen should be constantly watched. I'm worried that at night when he goes to the bathroom, he might fall. He is truly a brilliant, philosophical man. I am certainly glad and excited to get to know him more.

February 12

8:00 *He woke up and said he was not feeling well and then he went to the bathroom and VOMITTED. After cleaning up I gave him his Morning medication.*

8:30 *He went back to sleep.*

9:35 *Margaret called and asked how he was doing...I explained his vomiting...she said it's probably because he's been missing the 2 a.m. anti-emetic medicine.*

10:35 *Margaret said she was coming Wednesday 1 p.m.*

10:40 *Bob called, he'll come to fix the phone.*

10:45 *Elyse called. I suggested that I prepare a 2.5 ml anti-emetic medicine and place it in a glass by the alarm clock, which will be set at 2 a.m. so that he'll remember to take it.*

10:55 *Mansfield woke up and had a glass of Ultimate Meal and 4 strawberries.*

12:50 *He woke up and we talked. He wants to go to the bathroom...*

2:00 *He woke up and had Bloody OJ, 2 strawberries, and I gave him his anti-emetic.*

3:15 *He woke up after Elyse called.*

3:35 *He cooked his own Wheateena meal.*

4:00 *He VOMITTED...TWICE after eating only 4 spoonfuls of Wheateena.*

4:05 *He insists on CLEANING UP HIMSELF. I offered but he refused.*

February 14

7:38 *Wednesday Valentines I arrived early. He was awake. He was cooking his own breakfast. I was worried but he looked a lot more alert today.*

8:02 *He drank his 8am medication.*

9:08 *He went to sleep in the other room and said that he*

wanted to have the phone in there to answer it. I told him he does have another extension phone there. He slept.

10:00 I refilled his anti-emetic medicine.

10:15 Fran came. She talked to him a lot. It seems like a really good day today. He was sharp and very lucid. They talked about friends and memories.

11:30 He wanted to sleep again. He told Fran to buy a shaver, a list of stuff like Water, etc...He ate ½ cup of yogurt. And Fran left.

12:35 Fran came back with the Norelco and groceries. I started vacuuming.

1:10 Margaret came. Mansfield had a list of questions. He wanted to know about his physical condition. How to deal with it. He was very alert. He wanted to know about his sudden episodes. Margaret told him that he didn't have epilepsy...but he insisted...Margaret answered very professionally. It showed her 20-year experience. She was thorough yet very sensitive about the whole issue.

2:05 Margaret left after refilling the Med set. I gave him his anti-emetic medicine.

2:15 She left. Mansfield started shaving his head. I finished vacuuming his two bedrooms.

2:25 Emma called. They talked and he started crying. She's visiting Friday after arriving from University of Chicago tomorrow.

2:40 I offered lunch. He fixed his own bread with peanut butter and jelly, ½ banana, and five strawberries.

3:15 He rested while we talked a lot.

COMMENTS AND SUGGESTIONS According to Margaret of Hospice, it's common to have such a Good Day like today. But it can suddenly drop the next couple of days...or good days can stretch for 3 days and his energy level may drop afterwards. Anyway, let's savor

every sweet moment. Secondly, the anti-emetic medi-
cine application has definitely helped. And with our set
up of the alarm clock...I'm very happy that he's becom-
ing more and more independent and alert.

I checked in with Raymond, talking with him regularly, but reading these gave me an intimate sense of the
rhythm of Mansfield's days, the stream of visitors and
calls. In this brief time, he'd been visited by his girlfriend Elyse, old friends Bob, Andy, Ferenc, Jonathan
and Fran, and his daughter, Emma. Raymond's exacti-
tude in counting strawberries, and that he seemed to
genuinely like my brother, delighted me. I also felt he
prepared the way for me to live there. I anticipated
skirmishes with Mansfield. He hadn't told me he was
fiercely independent for no reason. I heard from Mansfield that Raymond was very nice and helpful, but too
intrusive. He complained of being followed everywhere
and his behavior examined minutely as if he were some
specimen of newly discovered insect.

I will find a way
to support the living

February 18, 2001

I fly back to San Francisco to live. I have agreement
from my employer to work in California for an unspeci-
fied period of time. My recent acquaintance, Paul, is
happy to live in my place and care for my two cats until
whenever I return. I have a new laptop that has been set
up to connect me with the data sources I need to do my
work remotely. In this almost magical interlude, the idea
has taken root in me that it must be possible to live life

fully up until the moment of death. I don't know what this might mean, but there is the sense that there has to be a way to support whatever sort of life wants to live itself. There is something important about continuity, about being among the things that support one's life and are imbued with one's own history. A few days ago, Mansfield said to me, almost in warning, "I'm ferociously independent. Inflexible. I notice you are socially engaged. I am not. I am intolerant. I have no tolerance for TV or humanity, even though I love humanity. This could be brilliant for both of us. In this particular form: you are you, me being me, going through our lives this way. There are unpredictable turns not always bad. There are sweetnesses." Not long before the new year, he had said, "The inevitability of dying is like a meditation —I contemplate it. I go back over my life all the time, like I'm assessing it: this is the way this life has dealt with the universe." I wonder how well that could be done in a hospital. This idea of providing him the safety and comfort of the familiar eclipsed my need to deny my brother is dying. But I was aware that it could be another trick of the mind and that somewhere I still held on to the possibility of a miracle, something that still might avert this reality.

Making myself a home

February 18, 2001

I make myself a monk's cell in the back bedroom. It is edifying work, vacuuming the old wall-to-wall carpet until I'm in a sweat, washing the high casement windows. I work with what is available, which is very little.

Since the time of his diagnosis, Mansfield has steadily given his possessions away. Books, furniture, CDs, then his own artwork, eventually beloved Buddhas and Hindu sculptures collected over the years, and finally even his sax—all were fanned out among his friends. His impulse was to pare down to essentials, to be increasingly unencumbered, as though he instinctively wanted to free himself from what held him here. In this empty square box of a room, I focus on creating only what I must have: something to sleep on, light, a small workspace. I find a three-fold cotton pallet that becomes my bed at night and folds up into a neat square during the day. It can be put away in the closet or used as additional seating. In the opposite corner, three old wooden crates become a computer stand and shelving for files. I requisition a large foam pillow from Mansfield's mound in the living room that I double up to wedge myself between wall and computer in the corner. I can sit either cross-legged, squatting, or sprawled if my legs start to get stiff. There is one small lamp on the floor by my bed and a clip-on light attached to the crate in my work corner. The room is satisfyingly spartan and utilitarian, like living aboard a small ship.

Mansfield's kitchen is a testament to months of self-medication. He put the wrong implements on the stove, left pots on long after they should have been turned off. The entire kitchen is covered in tiny filaments of melted black plastic that became airborne in the heat and attached themselves everywhere. They make a dark oily smudge and have to be scoured, which only intensifies their blackness before they finally disappear. I scrub the kitchen down, walls, cabinets, counters and floor, and clean the bathroom.

The monotony of the work allows me to muse. I recall a conversation Mansfield and I had over the phone before I came to live with him. He told me about a vivid dream he had had where he and Dad and I drove around and around in a complicated city looking for a place to park. It was one of those unrelentingly anxious dreams, where the dilemma persists, the outcome is always uncertain, always just ahead. "But I knew from this dream that you both would take care of me," he said. I felt pierced by his vulnerability, the relief he had found in this interpretation. And I felt the ephemeral nature of the pact with our father, as he had died suddenly, eight months earlier, with masterful grace, as though he made a decision and orchestrated it with clean dispatch in a matter of days.

I thought about my younger brother David, who was fully engaged with work and family in Maine. The same was true for my much younger sister Robin in Wyoming. I realized that I experienced my own life as having a more provisional quality. At 50, I nursed a low-grade yet pervasive dissatisfaction with my work and personal life, even where I lived, in a beautiful 100-year-old schoolhouse in Somerville, Massachusetts. I realized I was relieved to have distance from the man I had been seeing for two years. I was grateful that just then I was serving as a liaison between a group of speakers and their corporate, government, university and non-profit audiences around the world. Since I had reason to work at any hour of the day or night, I could do so from anywhere. My only problem was a new secretary in Boston who felt free to call me at 6:00 a.m. because that was the start of her workday on the East Coast. But that could be managed. I felt held by the web of people who loved my brother and who wanted to spend time with him—and they were not just here—the ones I'd met or knew—but were spread out around the world.

Getting my bearings in
an ever-narrowing orbit

February 20, 2001

My days are filled with attention to making small choices, like whether to have salmon and peas or beef franks and corn, Vernors Ginger Ale or tea, hot cereal or cold. These are Mansfield's staples, which keep appearing in his big blocky letters in brightly colored inks on the myriad small notepads on the kitchen counter. It is fun to cater to him because before his nausea was managed, he could only eat strawberries, yogurt and protein drink without throwing up. He has fresh pleasure in food. There is something satisfying in experiencing these small domesticities as joint choices, after living alone for so long. Each decision feels like an accruing: what appeals to Mansfield today? What can he imagine would delight his senses now? I find I want his every whim to be satisfied, his slightest desire fulfilled, as if there is an intelligence, which, if attended to closely enough, will feed him more life.

These small concerns stand in high relief against the backdrop of sleep. Mansfield sleeps all the time. He reported this to me on the phone, more than a year ago, with a kind of amazement in his voice that it was possible. He complained that it was like inhabiting a netherworld where all the usual bearings in his life dissolved and there was no landscape but the four walls of his apartment. At first, he held on by keeping up, in his usual way, with what everyone was doing. He would report on the goings-on in all his friends' lives—as though he took sustenance from their living. Just before I came to live with him, he warned me matter-of-factly:

"I love people and am gregarious but, as a general rule, I go to sleep—all the time."

Now I understand it. It is alarming to watch him sleep for hours in the morning, then awaken and be able to sit up for only one hour before needing to sleep again for another five hours. During the day I am working in the back room, on the phone or computer constantly. But at night I long for conversation with him, with friends. The time difference makes talking with friends in Boston only an occasional event. Mansfield had warned me that he could not tolerate TV or radio. He has no patience for any of the content, and the noise, even at a distance, grates on him. I think I can't bear it when he wants to go to sleep for the night at 8:00 p.m. I want to protest and argue and beg with his sleep. I want him to be up and talking. I try not to show my disappointment, as though I can swallow it with the same resignation he has. I find myself getting angry at his sleep: that is when the silent workings of his body implacably move toward his death, gaining in small increments that accumulate against his vitality, lucidity, joy and wit. In defeat, I relegate myself to reading through a shopping bag full of true crime books I stole from my friend's brother's garage. Night after night I read them for hours on end, until I finally disgust myself and have to throw them out.

I alternately rebel at, am terrified by, and take refuge in my own diminished existence as I modify my habits to match his. I sneak out during the day as he sleeps and run along the inland waterway behind the Dipsea Restaurant, where the egrets often appear, startling white ovals suspended amid the rushes. At night, when I can't stand it anymore, I drive into the center of town and visit the Depot Café, which sits at the delta of a small tree-lined plaza, and peruse books and magazines, or wander the many small shops that line the square, just to be out among people and activity. Sometimes, I wake up mid-step to a pervasive alarm at how small my life has become. But I feel tethered by a hovering apprehension that he could be up and there is no one to look out for him.

The extent to which this is so just revealed itself. My friend Marie invited me to a house-warming party for a colleague in Mill Valley. I consulted with Mansfield about what is appropriate wear in San Francisco. Marie and I find the house nestled into the steep hill above the main cross street in town. We enter to find a throng of people throughout the bright, multi-leveled house, many with young kids in tow. There is a crisp promise in the air, animated conversation and high spirits everywhere. I become acutely aware of feeling utterly separate from this. I am reminded that I inhabit dark, very quiet days, the telephone my only lifeline to a larger world. And I am 50, not 30. I worry about the rightness and viability of my work as compared with the shiny, fresh-faced potential I see all around me. When asked what I am doing in San Francisco, I find myself groping for words, awkward and apologetic to be bringing up dying in this scintillating atmosphere, knowing someone's sympathy might reduce me to tears in a matter of seconds. I feel an excruciating inadequacy, like someone who discovers they have worn the wrong dress to the ball. I leave as soon as I can and, rooting around on the dark walkway outside the front door, manage to walk away in someone else's shoes.

On weekends, I am able to get away to visit my friends Joanne and Marie and Marie's brother Kev in San Francisco, occasionally Dolores in Vallejo and once Amory near Sacramento. It is a treasured respite to be among the not-dying, but even in my walking to a restaurant, mediating disputes between Marie and her brother, or shopping at Jeremy's, the high-end thrift store south of Market, a part of my mind is always oriented to how Mansfield is doing, what I can get for him, what he needs. This even though I know he is with his partner, Elyse, who regularly enables me to get away.

Elyse, Mansfield's long time life partner

February 22, 2001

Elyse comes every few days, and I am so glad to see her that I am bursting with conversation. She brings a special meal, and we sit around the low table, sometimes reading from something Mansfield had written, sometimes telling stories. Though they have been a couple for years, Elyse still keeps her apartment in Noe Valley, acquiescing to Mansfield's need for absolute independence. I have to watch that I don't forget they need time by themselves. It is easy for me to want to stay and talk, forgetting that Mansfield's time awake is so limited. Elyse tells me that sometimes when I've left, he wants to get back into bed only 30 minutes later, leaving her feeling bereft. No doubt my presence is a relief to her at some level, reassuring her that he is safe without her having to drop everything and make the trip from Noe Valley, as she has done so many times. I am chagrinned to see how my social hunger makes me obtuse, makes me not recognize how she misses the privacy with Mansfield she used to enjoy as a matter of course before I came on the scene.

I first met Elyse two years ago at a rare family gathering precipitated by Mansfield's illness and his message that we all should come sooner rather than later. She was the consummate host, easing us through the shock of beholding his new gaunt frailty. She had a kind of classic beauty: lithe and auburn-haired with perfect features cultivated over generations in French New Orleans. She had a slight southern drawl that was at once languorous and aristocratic. Mansfield leaned on her, literally and figuratively as a kind of existential sustenance. In one picture from that day in Tiburon, they stand against a fence with the bay behind, and there's a physical comfort in how she fits against his chest, within his encircling arm. Her face shines with the pleasure of being in his embrace. She told me that when he went into the hospital for the first time, he asked her to stay with him, which she couldn't do. Then in his delirium following the ravaging chemotherapy, he called her often and begged her to come be with him. He told her he wanted her at his side when he died and asked her if she would be there. She said to me that day that after 20 years of his fierce independence and sometimes thoughtless exclusion of her, the acknowledgement of her importance to him, despite the circumstances, was gratifying. There was sweetness in his desire for her comforting, for her knowing how to handle a group of unfamiliar people who were family and who had descended all at once into the heart of a diminished existence, causing upheaval, over-stimulation, and exhaustion.

I had heard about Elyse for at least 15 years before I met her. On the telephone, Mansfield would say, "Guess what I'm about to do?" I'd say, "What?" "See ELYSE!" he'd say, with the enthusiasm of a young boy, his tongue curling around her name in a kind of anticipatory relish. "She's on the Golden Gate headed this way as we speak!" One story from their earlier years stays with me because of the particular way he told it. He described a Sunday morning when he still lived in the city, going out to pick up a paper, and seeing a stunningly beautiful couple. He said they were clearly fresh from a night of lovemaking, still brushing up against one another, fingers interlocking with a random familiarity. She was exquisite, perfect in her post-coital glow. And he proud and handsome like a Nordic god. "And guess who it was?" he asked. "I don't know," I said, expecting him to name a famous couple. "It was Elyse!" And again, he said her name as though savoring the moment that he was exquisitely skewered with recognition, appreciation, and a searing flash of jealousy. This was part of the delicate balance he practiced, born of the sexual mores of the time, his love for her, and his equally complete insistence on his own autonomy. He paid for that autonomy in painful separations of her instigation, but they found a way to remain a couple.

Elyse takes me in hand. I am grateful to her for showing me the ropes in so many small yet essential ways. She shows me the parking place by the school for the back entrance to the inland water walkway. She shows me where Mansfield likes to get take-out. One day, she takes me to the high-end grocery store in Sausalito. I've already been to the Safeway and the little corner store down the hill in Mill Valley, each within a tight radius from where he lives, which allows me to keep him in daily supplies, but she understands I might like something nicer, too. Somehow, despite how similar this Sausalito store is to where I shop at home, I feel anxious, like I'll never find my way around or learn how they do things here. I feel vulnerable and overly self-conscious. Everyone is smarter, faster, younger, fully engaged in their lives. I am afraid I'll get lost driving along the little side road parallel to 101 between Sausalito and Mill Valley, although I can't explain exactly how, because it seems impossible. It is as though my threshold for the new and unknown has just been exceeded. I have learned where he gets Chinese in Mill Valley and what he likes; where he gets Osso Bucco and that he likes it without the red sauce, about the little Indian place tucked away on the side road, and which fish place he prefers in Sausalito. But just now it gets to the quick of me and I feel raw and exposed. I realize I am far from home, uncertain about my role or the duration of my stay and terrified to face what is coming.

I discover, weeks after I set up my room, that Elyse had lobbied hard to be able to bring me a school chair—an old-fashioned seat with attached writing surface that she saw would make my workspace more comfortable. Mansfield would not allow it, insisting that nothing extraneous be brought into his space. His stance was so adamant that she'd left in tears.

We find a rhythm and I settle in

February 26, 2001

Earlier, in a telephone conversation from Boston, I had tried to pin Margaret down about Mansfield's changing condition and what she thought his prognosis was. She told me that it was impossible to say—he could go in a week or two or he could rally and live for months. That information contains everything. There is hope, no hope, some possibility for planning and the need to hold everything wide open. It has the effect of riveting the attention in the present: there is just this moment, this conversation, this cup of tea to make, this light in the sky.

It rains interminably. This does make it easier to spend so much time inside, as though the earth itself is tempering me for this diminished existence. The smaller sphere of life is made bearable as the urge to be outside is replaced with contemplative musings, teacup in hand, and the absorption of watching rain from inside—like watching a contained fire from the comfort of your favorite chair. Finally, I complain to Mansfield that it feels like it will never end. He says that after months and months of utter dryness this feels like a balm feeding the earth. The sound of it, the smell of it, the gloom of it brings him deep contentment. He is profoundly grateful for it.

We make a new ritual. When Mansfield lost all his hair in the early chemo treatments, he discovered that women were attracted to his baldness. He described one occasion when he met an old friend while leaving the Safeway who exclaimed, "Mansfield! You look fantastic! What are you doing?" He had paused, pointed his finger up to indicate the profundity of what he was about to say, and pronounced, "Dying!" and burst into laughter. Thereafter he shaved his head religiously. In his recent medicated lassitude, he had allowed it to grow back, which it did in patches. Since he is starting to gain strength from being able to eat again, he can stay awake a bit longer after breakfast. He sits backwards astride a swivel chair and leans his arms on the backrest. Standing behind him, I run the electric shaver up and over his head with a meditative regularity until it is perfectly smooth. There is something about the morning light, the small buzzing sound, or maybe the vibrating and lazy path of the whirring discs over his head, which give him an absorbing relief. Maybe it is just finally sitting up after endless hours of sleep. We open the curtains and move him closer to the window so we can both watch the workmen building houses across the way. We make up stories about them to give dimension to the landscape of our day. My favorite is someone we both call "My Man," a graying and physically fit man who moves with authority and a quiet self-respect. We speculate he might be the foreman on the job. According to us, he is a master at his craft who loves his work and is in high demand. He is a man's man, even though he has this dignity that sets him apart. We give him a loving wife at home but acknowledge that all women naturally appreciate him. We worry and conjecture if he doesn't show up for a day, and my heart secretly gladdens when I finally see him again. We agree that he is suitable for me.

Plumbing

February 28, 2001

I discover that the plumbing for Mansfield's unit is unreliable and that the same is true of the plumbing in his body. His medications compact his system, requiring him to take stool softeners. When he was self-medicating, he took them at random, doing so only when he felt the need. These two phenomena converge when I find an enormous turd—probably four days' worth—completely clogging the feeble toilet. I flush and flush to no effect, and fret at the problem that is not going to go away. Finally, I cross over into a mother's pragmatism. I quickly conceive what every dog owner knows and find a plastic bag large enough to keep the water out. I reach down and pluck the turd intact—surprisingly dense and firm—from the bowl. I fold it and wrap it in innumerable plastic bags until it is an unrecognizable lump of refuse and take it out to the garbage dumpster in the back. I feel remarkably accomplished that I have dispatched it so neatly and all without disturbing Mansfield's sleep, sparing him the indignity of having to witness it himself.

Later, I remember an experiment we conducted secretly when we were small—maybe 3 and 5 years old. One day when we determined our parents were occupied elsewhere, we carefully laid out toilet paper on the floor next to the toilet. We both took turns, squatting and defecating neatly onto the papered floor. This allowed the other to get down on hands and knees and peer up to see what exactly was happening there. We each witnessed the almost imperceptible sphincter open and keep expanding amazingly before quickly squeezing shut again. We found this satisfyingly instructive and were able to clean it up without our parents ever being the wiser—another kind of satisfaction.

Evening

March 2, 2001

Dusk is a sentient hour for Mansfield. We sit on pillows at the low table, finishing dinner. The construction workers are long gone and quiet descends on the neighborhood. Sometimes Mansfield reads to me from one of his manuscripts, or we tell stories. Often, we watch the eucalyptus blackening against the deep sky, the light turning until its presence and absence are equally balanced, and the world goes inside out. The massive Marin headland across the valley becomes a flimsy prop; the real workings of the universe are revealed as complex dimensions usually obscured and only now, in the moment of this turning, apprehensible. In the deepening light, what before was just the unremarked space between eye and distant tree, now has palpable depth, filled with intricately interwoven angulations. Then, all is right with the universe: my brother's dying, the two small deer walking in the street below. Everything is in its place—the echelons of memory, all possible futures—all is contained in this present and converges in a simple joy, a contentedness of the heart. In the distance, down in the valley, a lone drum sounds, as if it always had been there, merely emerging, momentarily, to consciousness in the crossing to night, like one might momentarily become aware of the sound of one's own heartbeat.

We clear the dishes to play solitaire. Not double solitaire or Russian Bank, but each our own game, because he says he wants to play at his own pace. We remind each other of games of rummy with our grandmother on winter afternoons in Windsor, Vermont around the small green felt-lined table. We would be huddled concentrating and chatting in a pool of lamp light against the fading afternoon. I look over and notice that the game Mansfield is playing now is not solitaire, but his own creation. He flips cards up in a long succession, then does a string of them all turned down in a wide arc before him. There is a slow rhythm in the movement of his arm. He has a contemplative focus, watching each card as it is turned, and appears utterly content. I feel a twinge of disappointment that he cannot play against me: in the fullness of this moment, I realize he never will again.

He tells me a story. There was a time, early in his business, when he painted a house in Sausalito. It was owned by a distinguished Hungarian man. He had married a woman who lived on the property perched on the steep hill above his home, whom he had gotten to know chatting over the fence. Years after working there, Mansfield received an invitation to the man's memorial service. He went, mystified as to why he was there, standing in his signature white among strangers. The wife spoke and, to his astonishment, acknowledged Mansfield. She said that while he was in their house, Mansfield's interest in her husband had brought him alive to the stories of his youth and homeland. She said she had never heard these stories before and never would have known about this time in her husband's life had it not been for the curiosity, respect and appreciation Mansfield showed him.

Fran,
friend and mentor

March 5, 2001

Fran comes in the morning. She brings flowers from her garden in Alameda. They are so unexpected in early March to my Bostonian sensibilities that the generosity feels extravagant, almost unbearable, like some part of me wants to flinch away rather than look and see what I have been missing all these long months. She puts them in a coffee can on the low table, almost carelessly. Sitting clustered there, they seem to absorb all the light from the gray sky and send it back out as supersaturated pinks and yellows and oranges and creams. Over the course of a few hours the fat globes relax open into embarrassingly voluptuous whorls, radiating the promise of sun, warmth and new things to come.

Though I have heard about Fran for years, I only met

her just before the first group meeting with Margaret. When Mansfield still didn't recognize me, it felt as though Fran comforted him and allowed him to swim up through his confusion, her familiar presence a sure ally as he struggled to orient himself. I knew from Mansfield's stories that she was an early mentor of his, teaching him silk-screening, which he embraced with his usual feverish enthusiasm. This new discipline precipitated a flowering of creativity as he saw the potential reach of his artwork expand. Fran and her partner Gary were some of the original family in the Glen Canyon and Surrey Street group houses, and Mansfield became like an uncle to Fran's son, David. Whenever he spoke of her it was as of a cherished friend and respected colleague.

Like Elyse, Fran knows Mansfield's habits. She knew him when he cooked hamburgers for breakfast; when, to claim his starving artist credentials, he ate dog food from the can when his money ran out; when he worked into the early hours of the morning, then fell asleep amidst the chemicals in his studio. ("I didn't tell him to do that!" she would protest.) She knows he likes certain soups, has to have Vernors Ginger Ale. There is a comfort in this familiar pragmatism that helps order life as though it will go on forever, as though, with this degree of specificity and knowledge, every moment holds everything in timeless ritual. Mansfield looks forward to Fran's visit and plans his sleeping so that he can spend his best awake hours with her. They are old appreciators of one another and can laugh and tell stories endlessly.

At first, I feel a bit intimidated by Fran. Her short, red, asymmetrical bob is daring and hip. She is warm, dark, and can immediately point out the absurd and ridiculous in a way that infects everyone and makes them relax and laugh. I feel by comparison my own quavering—the familiar faltering of spirit like a small squall coming through. I am able to hold this in abeyance, but it registers as a kind of stiltedness.

When Mansfield gets back in bed after his brief interlude awake, Fran and I retreat to the back bedroom, which serves as his office. She sits on the wooden banker's chair at his desk and I nearby on a free-rolling office chair mired in the rug. In the darkened room we begin a muted conversation, so as not to disturb his sleep. There is nothing familiar between us—and no tea or coffee or waitresses to order from or passers-by to gaze at—and I feel myself groping, as though rock climbing for the first time. It is, for me, an awkward labored conversation, and yet somehow, something in Fran's presence makes me more myself, and we have the beginnings of a friendship. Fran tells me that back when she was just starting out in L.A., she hung a large self-portrait, nude, over the street-level entrance to her studio. At the age of 59, she has a good belly laugh at her own youthful brass.

Margaret and Mansfield's rallying

March 6, 2001

Margaret, Mansfield, Elyse, Fran and I hold another meeting about medications. Since Mansfield has stabilized so well on the original regimen, Margaret wants to fine-tune it. We take notes describing each symptom, which drug it requires, that drug's physical effects on him and the frequency with which it could be administered. Everything is accounted for: Ativan, DSS stool softener, the pink anti-emetic liquid and syringes, Oxycontin patches. We draw charts in big blocky letters showing medication dosage and timing and post it on the kitchen wall. Any helper can look at the timetable or consult the notes for a specific symptom. At first the amount of information is overwhelming and requires riffling through pages of notes to match an urgent symptom with the right antidote. But it quickly becomes more manageable as anti-emetic syringes are filled in advance to the right dose and stored in the refrigerator, the medset is filled weekly, and pain pills or patches are meted out on schedule.

Margaret's presence has a powerful effect on Mansfield. Just before I moved to Mill Valley, he said to me on the phone, "Rational discretion empowers you." I can see that her still, calm presence embodies that. She feels like a lifeline in the maelstrom of pain, fear, uncertainty and confusion that attend his physical state. With a nurse's instinct, she knows that timing is important, that when she says she will arrive at 2:00, Mansfield will have carefully managed the balance of his energy between sleep and awake time so that he can sit up and talk with her at 2:00, so she arrives on time. She can explain what is happening in the overall processes of his disease, and in the specific instance he is dealing with, at a level of detail and specificity that conveys mastery and gives him choices. There is something to do to alleviate pain and suffering and it is logical and, invariably, it works as she says it will. She can make a suggestion, get on the phone, and a new array of drugs will appear, often within hours, that have the desired effect.

She is the conduit through which Dr. Pond presides over Mansfield's care from afar. She knows the systems of the body and she works the system of medical care to deliver comfort, support and a more tolerable existence. She is compassionate and encouraging; she embodies the kind of equilibrium that Mansfield seeks. That she lived more than 30 years before as part of the Diggers community in San Francisco, the radical communitarians who dispensed free food, medical care and housing, only elevates her further in his estimation. The respect he accords her gives her license to push him: she encourages him to get a hospital bed that will allow him to vary his position and the pressure points on his body over the long hours of sleep. He refuses. She suggests he get a special chair to make his shower taking safer. He allows it into the house, takes one look and laughs at it, relegating it permanently to the back bedroom closet. She ordered a wide crook-necked plastic container we have no idea what to do with, so just set it aside.

Mansfield begins to rally. Since the meds are regular, his pain is managed. He is not hallucinating from overdoses of anti-emetic, Ativan or Oxycontin. It feels like a Prague Spring, a sudden flourishing of the freedom of his old self against all odds. He wants to go to the tanning salon. When the weather clears, however tentatively, he wants to sit outside. One morning, he decides we should do a road trip. We gather meds, sick bag, everything we need, and in the fresh sunny morning air head north on 101. We drive past the scrub hills of Larkspur and Corte Madera. I haven't been north yet, and don't know where we are going or what landmarks to look for. We pass by the early San Rafael exits. I look over to ask Mansfield and see that he has nodded out, his chin on his chest and eyes closed. He sways with the movement of the car, oblivious to me.

"Mansfield," I say. "Where are we going?

His eyes open obediently for a moment, staring vacantly, then softly close again. I feel the old panic come over me, the fear of being lost in the universe, unable to find anything familiar and unable to get off an increasingly complicated and fast highway. As we sail past exit after exit, I grip the wheel in an effort to calm myself, dry my sweaty palms and quiet my heart.

"Mansfield!" I say urgently, "Where do you want to go?"

He is startled and looks up. He turns to me and a big smile fills his face. He reaches over and pats my leg comfortingly.

"I'm wit choo!" he says, as though in that moment he sees my fear and moves to diffuse it with his silly comment. His head nods again, and he is gone. In my anguish at seeing him move to take care of me, my panic dissolves. We are two people heading north on a sunny morning, one driving, the other asleep. That is enough.

Independence

March 7, 2001

Mansfield's newfound enthusiasm for life poses a dilemma for me. I have lived by the Calvinist notion of work and time, like an old workhorse in its traces from too early an age. This is so even as I continue to question my level of commitment to the work I do, representing organizational learning speakers and facilitators around the world. I bristle at authority, then comply with expectations and find myself nursing low grade resentment – at myself and at those above me.

But now it is clear to me that the rhythms of living and dying occur in another universe, altogether unencumbered by the arbitrary time strictures of an office. As Mansfield gains strength and wants to visit the sun beds at 10:00 a.m. ("My best joy!" he declares), I cannot tell him that he has to wait until my lunch break. And, of course, my lunch break in California will be 3:00 p.m. in Boston, where my colleagues are hard at work. I quickly decide that, because of his condition, we will do whatever he is inclined to do, whenever he is inclined to do it. This is simple, natural and the only possible response. The fact that the geographical range of my clients means I can easily work at any hour of the day or night helps me justify it. So, in this newly claimed freedom, we find ourselves driving desultorily up the corkscrew Camino Alto—the back way between Mill Valley and Larkspur—in the pristine morning sun. We swing by the post office, empty at mid-morning, then head over to the sun beds. They all know Mansfield there and treat him as a regular, so he can be his expansive self, a little swagger in his step. He casually asks how they and others who are not on duty are doing – as though it is just another moment of social banter on a quick trip, rather than a planned and cherished outing. He loves being tanned, but also the heat all around him is deeply comforting and takes him out of the relentless tedium of endless days of drugged sleep on his mattress. We go home and he crawls, exhausted, back under the comforter, well-toasted and content, banked by mountains of maroon, blue and purple pillows.

The Norwich News

March 8, 2001

Elyse comes early with a special meal for Mansfield. I bring out some files from a cache my younger brother and I had found in our father's office after his death, nine months ago. I had entertained the notion of creating a scrapbook with Mansfield and had collected photos accumulated over the last 45 years. In the moment, that impulse feels awkward, as if rudely suggesting a full and vibrant life can be reduced to a few keepsakes. But I want to show Elyse evidence of an early Mansfield exploit, *The Norwich News*, and I want to look at the papers again, myself. This was before Mansfield, when my brother was known as Alan Perkins, Editor.

I pull out the old copies, the type pale blue and almost disappearing, especially where the papers, now 40 years old, had been folded. Mansfield's energy is good, so we start to muse over them, reading aloud. Mansfield created *The Norwich News* when he was Alan Mansfield Perkins, a 10 year old, in 5th grade. Shortly after, he was joined by his classmate, Leonard, and later, Bill. It was an endlessly absorbing endeavor with weekly deadlines, equipment evolution to keep up with, young reporters to corral, the Carl Crow cartoon to be created for every issue, serial stories to write, illustrations to draw, the puzzle page to assemble and, of course, the ongoing question of what was news.

The mechanics of production were always changing. In the beginning printing was accomplished with a thin square dish filled with a gelatinous substance that somehow in a time-consuming labor-intensive process, transferred bluish letters onto paper. There were two or three next generations, each involving a redesign of the bedroom to accommodate the new equipment and supplies. Mansfield would angle a bookshelf out from the wall, creating a room within a room, and find neat nooks for typewriter, ditto machine (an early home copier), printing masters and other supplies. And there were appurtenances to buy: special paper, masters, developer fluid, and stamps for sending copies to distant subscribers— each of these requiring a specific request for money from our father. Along with the equipment, the format of the paper evolved from a few hand-printed pages to an 8-page typed, columned booklet.

Letters to our father were typed and signed Editor in Chief of *The Norwich News*, or Alan (editor):

```
Dear Daddy,

   I am always working on my room and chang-
ing it around. I have just finished moving
those two tables. The change turned out to
be a good one. Now I am working on making
shelves for the tables.
   Do you remember the gun that shot rubber
bullets you gave David? David really likes
it!
   As you know, Daddy Harry and Damma went on
a trip to Mexico. They will be back in
about three weeks. We just received a large
box from them with lots of Mexican things
inside. It is really fascinating.
   Will you please send me two dollars to buy
some fluid? I am taking good care of my new
shotgun.

Love,
Alan (editor)

P.S. I am getting low on stamps. If you
send me stamps this time, send three cent
ones (for second class mail).
```

The Norwich News undercut the competition by 2 cents at 5 cents an issue. It was distributed at the two local stores, Dan & Whit's and the IGA, for which it gave up 1 cent per copy. Mansfield kept graphs on his wall to tell him how much money he made on each edition. Coverage by the local competition (the Valley News and Vermont Life magazine)—with photos—gave him exposure and circulation grew to nearly 2000 with subscribers in places he'd never heard of. He advertised duplication services in the paper and looked for jobs on the side to supplement his income.

Content varied depending on the issues of the day and what the stable of fourth and fifth grade reporters and their sources (old friends, buddies and family) found newsworthy:

- Mrs. Gosselin is in the doghouse for starting a fire with the damper closed.
- NOTICE: Maps showing all the roads and residences by name are available for $1.00 at the Town Clerk's Office and the Dartmouth Book Store. This should be valuable to people making deliveries in town.
- NOTICE: Jillian Foley taught her dog to stand on its hind legs.
- Moving Rooms: Your Editor has changed rooms with his sister. Last Thursday in one hour he and his sister moved their rooms.
- After many years the Boston and Maine Railroad agreed to widen the Lewiston Bridge.
- Mark Logan would like any available material on Prehistoric Life. Call Norwich 647-R. (We laughed over this reminder of a time when there were only rotary phones and often, party lines.)
- Christmas Shopping: On the twenty-second and the twenty-third people may do their Christmas shopping in Hanover. On those days movies will be shown free.
- Turtles—Your Editor, Alan Perkins, found a painted turtle. He also found some interesting facts about one too. (a) males are similar to females but smaller (b) females dig a hole with their hind feet to put their eggs in. (from six to twelve eggs, white). (c) young do not emerge until spring (see picture).
- NORWICH NEWS HOLDS PARTY—As many of our readers know, The Norwich News was first published in April 1959. The editor, Alan Perkins, thought that it would be nice to celebrate The Norwich News' first anniversary by having a party. Editor's note: WHEW! What a destructive party!

With *The Norwich News*, Mansfield demonstrated an early aptitude for order, discipline and steady industry over a period of years. From talking about *The Norwich News*, we cannot pass up the opportunity to discuss the TOP HAT. The TOP HAT was one of the manifestations of the ever-changing architecture of my brother's room. Our father had made for each of us our own wooden chest that we could put our stuff in and lock. There was genius in recognizing that children crave privacy, but Mansfield was the only one who put it to good use. One day, after much advance notice and amid great fanfare, he opened the TOP HAT STORE. When David and I, the only shoppers, were let in, he had transformed all the surfaces in his room to display counters. His primary merchandise was Halloween candy that had been locked up in his chest, untouched, for 3 or 4 months. Each piece had its own label: Heath Bar—25 cents. Since we had finished our own candy within a few days of Halloween and the holidays were long gone, this was a cornucopia in our own brother's bedroom. There was more. Mysterious envelopes marked BLING BLANG! Upon purchasing one I discovered he'd gone to the kitchen, mixed TANG and sugar and produced BLING BLANG! I bought a set of 3 X 5 cards for a report I had to do. When I got around to working on my report, I discovered the top and bottom cards were empty and the entire pack in between was written on. When I protested he couldn't help expressing his delight with his high maniacal laugh, enjoying the fact that I'd allowed myself to be so roundly fleeced. When things got out of hand like this, or demand waned out of satiation, or the fact that he already had all our money, or due to mid-winter boredom, the TOP HAT STORE would suddenly implacably close. It would open months later when he felt the time was right again.

The Artist

Since he'd started *The Norwich News* at 10, Mansfield had had a feverish creative energy. He took up painting in high school. On school vacations, he would set up his room as a painting studio and work intensively for hours on end. If we were visiting our father's house in Michigan, my younger brother David and I would steal hours in front of the forbidden TV, fully narcotized, while Mansfield blazed away on canvas in the next room. He had an instinct for discipline. He organized himself so that his energies flowed decisively in one direction.

Our mother was always passionate about the arts. She used to take us to play at the Cranbrook Academy of Art, a few miles from our house in Michigan, while she took a sculpture class or pursued her secret infatuation with a gay pianist, which would eventually lead to the dissolution of her marriage. She admired the Beats and jokingly disparaged her wealthy and generous older brother-in-law, whom she relied on financially throughout her life. With a righteous contempt camouflaging admiration, she declared him "so square he is a cube." It was only much later that we understood she was born into wealth, had roller-skated in the basement of the Drake Hotel with the Wrigley sisters when she was a child during the Depression. At the age of 50, she still had to vent her sense of personal affront that her father had refused to let her take her beloved horse to college with her.

There was a time—it was always near the end of day, in the endless Michigan summer twilight, when she would go to the piano. Her working piece was a Rakhmaninov piano piece—a recording of which I later found and sent to Mansfield, who cherished it, as I did. Mansfield and I and our younger brother, David, would crawl beneath the piano, our play focused by the crashing chords overhead. She would play it over and over, as though she never could get the tempestuous passion of it quite right. There was the perfect lyrical symmetry of the first lines, like two follow-on statements leading to an explanation neatly tied up, then the abrupt and seething answering lines. Somewhere in there she got hung up in the fingering and would go back to the beginning to approach it again and again. She was wrestling with finding herself trapped at 30 with three kids in the 1950s Michigan hickory flatness. We absorbed her conflict as a particular imprint of sound, vibration, and a timeless quality of light. Perhaps her frustration mirrored her own father's unfinished singing career, his serious aspirations set aside to make his way in the new world of machine tools, in order to support his growing family. Like a warning message on a car's rearview mirror, there was something more complicated than it appeared in what we experienced. At its simplest, we saw a spirit rebelling against the dull strictures of workaday necessity, a turning away from the expectations of convention cultivated by a long line of worthy forbears who included bankers, judges, mayors and farmers. She opted instead for what she saw as the true vitality and greater life of the imagination, following the impulse to paint, model clay, play the piano, write. The badge of poverty was to be worn with pride and as protest, as evidence of genius and a closer proximity to a vague God. Poverty would be compensated for in recognition and respect, perhaps immorality.

Mansfield was steeped in this attitude, and it found perfect expression on the stage offered by the Zeitgeist of the '60s. He arrived in San Francisco in 1966. He was enrolled in the San Francisco Art Institute on Chestnut Street. After the first semester of dutifully attending classes, he left the school, swept up in the emerging impulse to chart a new way of living and determined to create a path of his own artistically. He would make his way on instinct, phenomenal discipline and love of hard work. This was a serious and heady experiment, individually and socially, and called for the rigorous spirit of the crusader. Under the early tutelage of his high school friend, Butterworth, he cut his baby teeth on the psychedelic drugs and cultural experiences that would signal an epochal upheaval in the status quo and come to define a generation. He soon became known as "Mansfield," his middle name, relegating the old shell of Alan Perkins to the East Coast and history. San Francisco was the locus of the movement's promise. The weather was benign, the Spanish name and architecture suggested exotic possibilities, and the middle class had vacated to the suburbs. So rent was dirt cheap. The time was ripe. Mansfield reported that, in his early days, there were maybe a few hundred like-minded co-conspirators poised on the cultural edge. Within less than a year, thousands of hippies would descend on the Haight from all over the country and inaugurate the Summer of Love.

Early on, Mansfield abandoned his painting to pursue the creation of a series of entirely white Plaster-of-Paris and fiberglass torso sculptures embellished with hair of rope and twine and found objects such as recording tape, piano keys, and pieces of broken oboe or violin. Most often, the castings were taken from his girlfriend, Betty. The White Sculptures began to get recognition. They were written up in the *San Francisco Chronicle*, shown alongside Annie Leibovitz's early photographs of Mick Jagger, Janis Joplin and Carlos Santana at the Sun Gallery, and in one-man shows at The Three Voids, The Emperor's Gate and the Lucien Labaudt Gallery. Many of the sculptures were hung in Pacific Heights mansions and even built into yachts. But Mansfield began to despise the art scene. An old friend, Gary, recounted the story of manning a booth at a fair for the Phoenix Gallery in Berkeley, which handled R. Crumb and other psychedelic and comics artists —probably in 1970. He was startled by a guy who strode up to him, asserting himself very forcefully. The guy introduced himself as Alan Perkins. "Mansfield," Gary observed, "was his greatest creation." Mansfield pronounced it outmoded, old-fashioned to be a gallery artist. He yearned to get out and touch people. He had no tolerance for any part of the commercial aspect of promoting his work. Witnessing the proliferation of genius music coming out of every crevice in the city, and finding ecstatic resonance in himself, in the teeming music halls of San Francisco, he became convinced that music was the revolutionary medium. He determined that he would make art for the musicians he loved and the public who listened to them.

By 1970, Mansfield's art had migrated to silk-screen printing, under his friend Fran's expert tutelage. The combination of fine craftsmanship, replicability and range of visual possibility in silk screening were fuel to his creative fire. He worked like a demon, a feverish alchemist who would exhaust himself and eventually fall asleep in his studio. He used high contrast photographic mandalas, producing a hybrid of psychedelic art infused with Tibetan Buddhist influences. Convinced the artist had to reach a mass audience, he did much of the promotional artwork for San Francisco's famous Keystone Korner Jazz Club, so named because it was situated opposite a North Beach police station. Mansfield aspired to create album covers for his favorite rock and jazz musicians, but he refused to submit his work through normal corporate channels, preferring instead to give his work directly to the artists as a gift. In keeping with the rules of the new renaissance, he categorically rejected authority, saw no reason to play with the suits. He did exactly what he wanted, the way he wanted, refusing to consider that he might pay for it in a lack of long-term recognition and success. His friend Jack argued with him endlessly, urging him to go to LA or New York and get an agent. But he refused, insisting on spending the bulk of his negligible income in creating, mounting and presenting his artwork directly, each piece an offering wrapped in an Indian print cloth. This was how he submitted his work to musicians he admired: Herbie Hancock, Cecil Taylor, Keith Jarrett, and Thelonius Monk, among many others. This impractical strategy was maddening to the friends who championed his capability and wanted a success for him that matched his talent and devotion.

Mansfield was not shy. He told tales of personal encounters, in the service of promoting his work, not only with iconic artists like Grace Slick, Ravi Shankar, Carlos Santana, and Robin Trower, but with Alan Watts, R. Crumb and his wife Aline, Allen Ginzberg, Timothy Leary and others. He knew the Hells Angels, Tiny, Cinque, and Willy Wolf of the Symbionese Liberation Army and China House in Berkeley long before Patty Hearst entered the picture. In addition to the few actual hits he got with McCoy Tyner, Mahavishnu Orchestra and ZZ Top, Mansfield was told his work hung in Miles Davis' hallway in New York City and countless other places.

🎵 🎵 🎵

Mansfield took up writing at the age of 42. There was a restless hiatus sometime after his 1985 ZZ Top Sleeping Bag Extended Play cover for their Afterburner album, when he put down his artwork and attempted to satisfy his creative impulse by playing his sax in regular music jams at Santulli's in Sausalito. He always reported the transcendent release he experienced there while disparaging his contribution as negligible, considering it his good fortune that his presence was tolerated among more serious musicians. He claimed he was incapable of working on his writing for only a few hours in the morning or at night, as, I told him, some successful writers did. Instead, he organized his life so that he ran his house painting business 12-14-hour days, 7-day weeks, for weeks on end with no breaks. Then, he'd take 2 or 3 months off, during which he would work at the same pace on his writing. He had an ascetic's devotion; nothing was as intensely absorbing as tending his fire. He generated energy from the rigor of this schedule. He would call periodically and exclaim at the almost hallucinatory effect of working so intensively within his own four walls, day after day. He would read his favorite passages, savoring a word or turn of phrase that particularly delighted him. He would report experiencing ecstasy, then bemoan the fact that he had waited so long to start and that he had so far to go to approach the quality of his early heroes, Naipaul and Rushdie.

My favorite piece was a collection of vignettes he called *Eden Warriors: Golden Age of the Counter-Culture* (unpublished). This early writing fit the exuberance of the times he described and had the sureness of a lived story. They were psychedelic road warrior tales of adventuring in the perpetual spring of the '60s—a kind of "meetings with remarkable men." They described encounters with the icons of the generation: musicians, poets, spiritual teachers and intellectual leaders, all of which take place against the backdrop of his own rhapsodic metaphysical conjecturing, sexual skirmishes and drug adventures. Even the places he described had a legendary ring: Keystone Korner, Esalen, Winterland, the Fillmore, the Avalon. The stories are told from the point of view of his various roles as artist, would-be musician, intellectual explorer, philosophical seeker and, for a while, drug purveyor. And they are a lens into a time when he and I were only sporadically in touch with one another, so I learned a lot about his life from them.

One of the *Eden Warrior* vignettes recounts his meeting the pianist McCoy Tyner at Keystone Korner. He described a rainy night, the throng of glistening squad cars across the way, flashing neon signs reflecting on the wet pavement. The club was already turning people away by the time he arrived, but he was allowed in, since he did their media coverage. He greeted the floor manager, barmaids, and bartender, whom he'd known for years, and shook hands with several friends he'd spotted, relishing his get-up in a pilot's jacket with three gold bands around the cuffs. Listening to John Coltrane piped through the P.A. system, he registered his appreciation for the refreshing sophistication of this music as compared with the huge, raging rock concerts, which he knew and loved so well. He mused on having seen

Weather Report, Miles Davis, Pharoah Sanders, and Alice Coltrane among others in this tiny club. He had pitched his work there to the "extraterrestrial" Sun Ra, "Bright Moments" Rahsaan Roland Kirk, and Larry Coryell's lovely wife who served as Coryell's manager.

Mansfield had entre into the backstage area, to which he strode with authority. He entered the quiet sanctuary of the long back office, papered with posters from former famous concerts, and approached Tyner, who exuded a steady, paternal authority (only 10 years Mansfield's senior, but with towering stature in the firmament of jazz musicians). Inspired by his music, Mansfield had spent weeks composing a silk-screen print that would reflect his sense of the majesty of Tyner's vision. As his ideas took form, a friend gave him an image of African tribesmen in ritual dress, arms upraised. He flipped the image, joining it to the original, creating a radially symmetrical mandala, which became the heart of the composition. Already the artwork had been reproduced as a poster and flooded throughout the streets of San Francisco, signaling the Tyner appearance at Keystone. In preparation for his encounter with Tyner, whom he knew to be a practicing Muslim, Mansfield had read the entire Koran, so that he could more deeply appreciate the whole man. He had excised brief passages imbued with Sufi resonance and quoted them in his letter of introduction. Todd Barkan, the Keystone manager, introduced them and they shook hands, a copy of Mansfield's proposed album cover mounted and positioned on the desk behind them. Tyner verified that Mansfield was the artist, thanked him for his effort, and declared his approval. He promised to push for the concept with the establishment at Fantasy Records, who, like all record companies, had their own stable of approved artists. They shook hands again as they became aware of the anticipatory hush in the audience.

Mansfield and Barkan slipped out to join the standing room only audience as Tyner appeared onstage to wild applause.

Mansfield's artwork graced the cover of the rare solo album that grew out of this concert, *Echoes of a Friend.* Released in late 1972, it was Tyner's homage to the guiding influence of the late John Coltrane, with whom he had collaborated for years before having a falling out, not long before Coltrane's death. One of the cuts on the record was Tyner's version of "A Love Supreme." Subsequently, Mansfield's cover artwork was voted Best Jazz Album Cover of the Year in Japan. In a haunting synchronicity with the album's title, the friend who had given Mansfield the image he used would soon take her own life. A lingering resonance remained forever associated with that image, the album title, the music and this early success. He was 23.

❊ ❊ ❊

When the catharsis of writing *Eden Warriors* was exhausted, Mansfield turned to reading Crichton and others, looking for a success formula, avid to find a voice that would be recognized. He experimented, concocting adventure stories rooted in his various friends' exploits: diamond running in Sierra Leone with sloe-eyed exotic beauties, ribald magic realism in Latin America, venture capitalists slick in the fast lane, an older man modeled after his friend Ferenc's father, with two achingly beautiful Asian women consorts. These would be peppered with philosophical disquisition—the setup being an adventurer happening upon an obscure rite that would open the door to lofty commentary. There would be a chance encounter with a mystical elder capable of initiating the hero into esoteric spiritual teachings, or an almost anthropological look at the origins of the drug culture. He would call his friends around the world to get convincing local details. He had a knack for storytelling, a kind of energy and exuberance that loped along at an engaging pace. There were moments of beautiful writing. And there was a prodigious output, with full manuscripts arriving regularly in the mail, either in thick tomes, or on floppy discs.

Invariably, though, a story with action and direction would detour sharply into an adolescent boy's sexual fantasy. This occurred even in a story of Jesus' lost sojourn in India, which I had to admire. Women had shining hair, tumbling locks, laughing arabesque eyes, ample breasts, perfect teeth, and hips that threatened to spawn civilizations. They had names like Aisha or Consuelo and never a distinctive personality. They were Armani-clad ice queens yearning, unbeknownst to themselves, for molten sexual release, or powerful earth goddesses whose pulchritude matched the riches of the Amazon River basin. The most voluptuous could turn suddenly and declaim knowledgably on Rajneesh. I would react to all this with rage and incredulity. Mansfield and I argued about it endlessly.

"They're not people!" I would protest. "Women don't have bouncing curls and almond or obsidian eyes. Your characters are cardboard figures. The minute they enter the scene I want to throw the manuscript across the room!" I had actually launched one bulky ream ten feet away from me in sheer disgust. "This is Betty and Veronica territory! I liked that when I was 10!"

"But my whole life is a cartoon," he'd counter. "Besides, I just talked with Jeff in LA and he loves them! Can't get enough of them!"

"And he's married to someone he thought was one of them, until he brought her over here and she started showing her true personality!" I reminded him. "Besides, it just doesn't convince me ... I don't really feel any of these people! I don't want to know them, and I really don't want to spend time with them. They aren't real!" But, in fact, so many of his outlandish characters were real: Zen Guy, or Paul, really was called Mr. Delicious Man. Lightnin', or Chris, really was Magnolia Thunderpussy's Fastest Delivery Man. And Jonathan really was called The Tusker.

Sometimes I would write a critique and fax or mail it to him. He would then declare me brilliant and a better writer than he in a way that would aggrandize me, based on a few sentences, and diminish him, glossing over his talent for storytelling and the considerable energy and love he put into his work. Then I would feel frustrated that we were both stuck in the same two-dimensional space his characters inhabited, with no place to go. In some way, it felt to me that the lifeblood of real feeling that could animate his characters and provide a unifying underlying structure was missing. What I could not square was that the women in his life—Elyse, Fran, Susan, Tereza and others—were complex, smart, accomplished, sophisticated, reflective, feeling people, with whom he had real relationships. His own daughter, who most closely approximated the cartoon Veronica good looks, was his intellectual equal, and the recipient of his deepest love and respect. I told him I liked best what he'd written from his own experience, that I admired how alive it felt. I asked why he didn't write about his painting crews, as the stories he told about them were vivid and astonishing. There was Orit, the Uzi-toting Israeli woman, John, the British man who married a woman whose house they'd painted; the Irish man in a tragic bind with the law. There were those clients who became friends: Bill, the venture capitalist, John and his wife Emily, and their daughter.

Our mother once critiqued his writing in a long and

scathing letter, which he prized. Less than a year before her death, she complained in a tongue-in-cheek letter to me that her attempts to induce him to read Anne Lamott and Alice Monroe were dismissed as simplistic "creative writing 101" and pretty dull, definitely losing out to his more "Bunuelian-inspired imagination." She reported that he had just decided his *nom de plume* would be the combination of their names, Joan Mansfield, crowing that she'd go down in history yet.

Mansfield's writing fed and tortured him. His appetite for immortality, for transcendence in the form of recognition for his work, was enormous. It was a formidable engine driving his feverish intensity and discipline. He boldly tried to sell his novels, when others might have waited to complete a few more drafts. As with his artwork, he didn't shrink from feedback from the world and yet often dismissed or ignored it. Over the years his writing became more refined despite his periodic protestations that it was all shit, that he was a sledgehammer in comparison to the subtle brilliance of an Arundhati Roy or Michael Ondaatje.

Through their mutual friend, Zen Guy, Mansfield submitted a piece of his to Pico Iyer for review. Iyer sent Mansfield a gentle note, praising certain qualities in his writing and making suggestions about ways he could improve. Mansfield was exultant. Yet, rather than taking Iyer's advice, he promptly excised the most glowing phrases, selectively quoting them out of their more sober context, in his next letters to publishers. I was apoplectic in my outrage, suggesting that he was not only misappropriating the subtlety he so admired and insulting the favor Iyer had rendered him, but also misrepresenting a respected writer's words in a way that would only reflect poorly on him. This, of course, did not deter him one whit, undoubtedly serving only as further evidence of my comparatively timid nature. And,

I had to admit that, though I didn't approve, I admired his instinct to assert himself.

Mansfield undertook a piece of writing that was a compound rendering of his most important early relationships, from an archetypically blinding high school crush on an unobtainable girl a few years older than he to the relationship that ended in his girlfriend Betty's death by suicide, some time after they had broken up for the last time. He considered this event the tragedy of his life—an experience of such deep pain that he was unsure he would ever emerge from it. When he did, after experiencing her wanting of him from beyond the grave, he said he understood that suicide could be the right choice for someone, when it offered release from an all-encompassing despair from which a person could not extricate herself. Mansfield and Betty had grown up together in San Francisco. With our father's help, they had bought a house in the Fillmore, from which they were ultimately run out by the very "brothers" with whom they thought they were showing solidarity. They managed to come through that hell together.

They'd also had two big dogs, making an early family of sorts for Mansfield. He created a special language for his dogs, which his friends were instructed in. He continued on occasion to speak their language and ostensibly consult their wisdom to the end of his life, long after they were gone. He was even exacting about the spelling and pronunciation of this language: the code name for his main dog was Maha Legum de Couda Dreg, only properly said with a kind of nasal inflection and stentorian tone. Betty was the muse for much of his early sculpture work, the contours of her beautiful face and shoulders emerging in white from a complex composition of flotsam and jetsam as though washed up on the beach or glimpsed in a dream. They had loved and betrayed each other in their exploration of what free love actually meant in practice. It was the times, or it was how the times intersected their particular fresh and exquisitely balanced vulnerabilities.

Finally, one of the infidelities broke his heart, even though he acquiescd to, witnessed, and actually encouraged it in the moment. Despite wanting to be on the forefront of breaking old mores, Mansfield no longer experienced it as experiment or free expression, but rather as a deep violation of his trust in her and their intimacy. Their relationship had always been volatile and tempestuous. With this breach, they began to drift apart, an uneasy and protracted separation.

Mansfield no doubt exhibited his particular implacability, a kind of infuriating imperviousness inherited from our grandfather. In the face of that, and despite her adventurous sexual proclivities, Betty clung to him as though she could not find her footing in the world without him. She would call from odd places at any hour. There would be no voice on the other end, but he could hear her breathing and would know it was she. It haunted him. Sometimes he would just talk into the silence to her until she hung up. Sometimes she would say she wanted his child. She was restless, returning to the East Coast where she had grown up, then moving back and forth across the country. She talked about going to Europe. They'd get back together, but it wouldn't work, and they'd separate again. Then, one night, he got a call and immediately knew it was about Betty. She had pulled a plastic bag over her head and suffocated herself. The only identification on her was a slip of paper with his telephone number. He was asked to come identify her, and that experience shook him to the core. In the weeks and months after her suicide, he was overwhelmed by a psycho-emotional onslaught including hyper-real dreams that she had returned and was crouched over his sleeping body, attempting to suffocate him so that he could rejoin her. He experienced his struggle as an exchange with a very real spirit, an appeasement and liberation of Betty's hungry ghost. He felt there was no sacrifice that could balance the injustice of her suicide, yet his liberation from its hold on him could be hers too. Seven years later, I received a letter from him describing the layers of grieving and expiation he was only then seeing in some perspective. Despite eventually having a love relationship with Elyse that lasted more than 20 years, he never lived with a woman again.

🌿 🌿 🌿

In about 1969, Mansfield initiated the first of two group houses he would preside over for many years. He ran the Glen Park house, 289 Surrey Street, for more than a decade. It became a gathering place for artists, poets, musicians and a steady stream of world travelers who knew it as a base of operations, a dependable way station where they would be welcomed and a place they could recommend to their friends. With three stories and a basement, a sloping yard, at least 9 bedrooms and 2 kitchens, there were generally 10 to 15 people living there. Mansfield was the reigning spirit of 289 Surrey Street; he rented it first, and he didn't leave. I suspect it was also known as his house because he had an implacable will and undoubtedly imposed house rules that would have made the long-term success of such an endeavor possible. It was here he was known to cook hamburgers for breakfast and occasionally eat dog food from the can when his funds ran low. Jam sessions at 4:00 every afternoon drew talented musicians from all over the city. The people associated with Glen Park would become Mansfield's life-long extended family:

Jack, Fran, Elyse, Bob, Jonathan, Dugan, Gary, Jeff, Susan, Paul, Lightnin', Zen Guy, Ferenc, and Andrew among many others.

And it was here he became known for some of the more maddening behaviors that became his signature. He reveled in prolonged interaction in his own domain with the friends he loved and respected, and would hang out endlessly and tirelessly, often being the last to go to bed. In a café or nightclub or even someone else's place, he was evanescent, showing up to touch base with his friends and then disappearing. He would be effusive in his praise for the scene, but invariably he would be out the door within 15 or 20 minutes. He was impatient, as if he could not tolerate being subject to someone else's timetable or small talk. He could be unrelenting in corralling his friends to do something he wanted to do, such as attending a Buddhist event at Fort Mason, but he was impervious to their entreaties for him to join them somewhere, or he'd show up briefly and then leave, as if he'd fulfilled his obligation just by appearing.

My only experience of one of his group houses was when I first met Emma while on a trip to San Francisco for work. Early in that visit, I experienced the culture shock of showing up at Mansfield's house dressed in the bland taupe suit my business school friends had insisted I buy that made me look like a 1950s stewardess. It was early evening and people were congregating for a jam session. Mansfield was warming up his sax, in the nude, running it up and down modal scales. People kept sticking their heads into the room where we were, to be introduced. I remember Dugan especially, as he was quite young, strikingly handsome and a gifted guitarist. Paul was there—a gentle and lovely man with bongos under his arm. I changed into my jeans as quickly as I could and wondered where I had gone wrong, to find myself an imposter in the buttoned-down business world when the possibility of this raw visceral life burgeoned all around me.

The next morning, we drove to Susan's house on Burroughs Street. Susan was the mother of Mansfield's daughter Emma. I had spoken with her on the phone many times, where she assumed the role of older sister, talking about the joys of having a child and encouraging me to do the same. She was even more vivacious and engaging in person and made a point of winning me over early by declaring that I was prettier than Mansfield was handsome because I had the more classic features. Emma was five at the time, a thin slip of energy with a keen face amidst a cascade of golden curls. She was dressed in a bright Mexican skirt that opened into a pinwheel of color as she careened around the back yard, playing with her father. I noticed, soon enough, that though Emma said little to me, she rarely took her eyes off me and somehow managed to continually insert herself between me and Mansfield, as if assuring that I would not take him away.

JOURNAL

Jean asks me about work

March 9, 2001

I bump into Jean, a neighbor of Mansfield's, whom I have met a few times coming or going from the apartment complex. In a brief chat, we discover that we both have experience working in executive search—which she is still doing. She casually asks me if I plan to stay in the Bay area and I'm startled to realize that I am so focused on Mansfield, it never occurred to me to even consider this. The idea intrigues me and feels unsettling. She suggests I could easily get back into the search business here. I remember well how much I loved interviewing people and writing their profiles, even if they were primarily focused on work. I recall the particular delight I felt when clients were surprised that they learned new things in my profiles about people they'd known and worked alongside for years. I remember the satisfaction of finding a right next step for someone that also matched an organization's need and the sense of high energy and promise all around. I remind myself that a close friend of mine in the Bay area is still in the business and happily doing well. Yet I also register a deep reservation, reminding myself of the tedium, the "dial for dollars" aspect of the business. And I know I would need to either work for someone else or develop my capacity and self-confidence in the sales process in a new market, to be able to attract work that was challenging and satisfying. I wasn't good at either one of those things. I distinctly recall my sense of relief when I left the business eight years ago. And yet, what about the weather here? There is snow on the ground in Boston. And then, what about the significant cost of living increase, when I thought Boston was already high? The question lingers in me.

There is a balm in the day-to-day companionship with Mansfield. I am fed by our ongoing conversation, his depth and brightness. It is easy and satisfying in a way I miss and want more of in my life. I also see, from this distance, how stultifying my workplace environment is. If I can do the work perfectly well from here, why return to that? And I revel in the climate and the beauty of the land here. It feels so much more open, inviting and adventurous than Boston. Is that because I am giving myself the time to look at it, to soak it in? Is it because I am doing so with Mansfield? A decent ocean beach is ten minutes from here, not an hour away in heavy traffic, as it is in Boston. The same is true of a walk in the Marin headlands. In a brief chat with my Brazilian colleague, Jose, I tell him why my brother's condition necessitates talking with him from a different time zone. Within moments he emails me an exquisite picture of his four-year-old daughter gazing into the camera in a white lace crinoline dress and black Mary Janes—as if to cheer me up by indicating that life indeed continues. It is a small sweetness that brings tears.

Margaret's Call

March 12, 2001

Margaret calls. She isn't just checking in, as she usually does. She tells me she thinks Mansfield's grace and dignity are exceptional. She says she finds his spirit, intelligence and acceptance of his situation to be rare. She says she considers it a privilege to know him. That is the whole conversation.

Early Tutelage

Mansfield always reveled in physical intensity, lying in the sun sweating after a game of tennis, playing on the beach for hours at The Devil's Slide when his daughter Emma was young, hiking the Tennessee Valley trails in the smell of the late afternoon air, the eucalyptus exhausting the heat of the day. In high school, when on vacations, he would set up a studio in his room and paint feverishly for long hours without a break, suffering no interruptions. When he was maybe 11, we were driving to our grandparent's place, known as The Farm, when we saw a deer in the field off to the left, where Mt. Ascutney rises up behind. He begged our mother to stop the car so he could sneak up on it. We all watched as the deer bolted and he chased it, running flat out for an impossible distance across the long field. When he finally came back, heaving and exhausted, he claimed to have entered a grotto in the woods where other deer were assembled. We were wide-eyed in wonder, and of course would never really know if it had actually happened.

Maybe this love of the physical came from the early and close tutelage of our grandfather. When we moved to Vermont, we lived only 20 miles from our grandparents' home. Visits to The Farm became a weekly ritual, and summer vacations often meant extended stays there without our mother. The trip was a long meander south on Route 5, taking an interminable amount of time through the small towns of Wilder, Hartland Four Corners, and Hartland into Windsor. Before either of the interstate highways were put in—on one of which Mansfield would work construction—it was a long excursion. Our grandfather, Daddy Harry, was at first a daunting figure. He had severe, chiseled features beneath a thick white brush cut and his word was law. A brief mention of his sharp stick and we were brought swiftly into line. The fact there was no sharp stick didn't matter. He was the only person we knew who made our mother cry, which we witnessed related to some disagreement about turning up the heat, when she no doubt seethed at finding herself, at 32, under his dominion once again, even if only temporarily. He was a man of iron discipline and daily ritual. We would hear him arising at 6:00 to go start the massive wood stove in the kitchen and set the coffee water going. He would then retreat to his bedroom only to reemerge after the rest of the family had congregated at 7:00. As others cleaned the kitchen, he was at his desk in the library doing paperwork. Then, after the dishes were done and the day's shopping list was ready, there was always a trip into town in the bed of his old maroon pickup truck. We vied for the best spot, which was always crammed back against the tailgate where we would feel the maximal impact of a series of bumps the pocked dirt road afforded and which we pleaded with our grandfather, at the top of our lungs, to hit head on. Once in town we took up residence in the comics section in the drug store while Daddy Harry went about his errands, being greeted with various, "Good morning, Mr. Beal"'s along the way. One time we had the luck to be present when he bumped into a friend of his who had descended from his remote hillside home wearing a leather helmet and driving a gleaming Excaliber. We were mesmerized by the exposed pipes, as speechless as Toad in *Wind in the Willows*. Proximity, birth order and gender gave Mansfield special standing with Daddy Harry. That Mansfield by the age of nine was without his father due to divorce and Daddy Harry had borne adulthood without a son helped forge their bond.

Daddy Harry dressed impeccably for the cocktail hour, a hallowed tradition at The Farm. Later, bronzed from winters in Mexico, he would appear clad in raw silk or cotton pants and shirt, often in surprising yellows, creams, pinks or greens. This was an unprecedented sight in Vermont but carried off with self-assurance and a commanding physical presence. We would be allowed to assist in the butler's pantry, helping him put out ice, olives, crushed, spiced bugs from Mexico to rim the glasses, different sized and shaped cut glasses and, most importantly, corn curls—those puffy orange things that could be eaten one after another to endless satisfaction throughout an adult conversation. All would be assembled and ready on trays. We would proceed to the library, where everyone congregated. Daddy Harry had to be in his favorite chair with everyone else arrayed around him before he would start to tell stories. These were adult tales meant to amuse and provoke, draw debate and stimulate conversation, which would go on at endless length, back and forth over our heads.

Often when we arrived at The Farm, Daddy Harry would be at work in one of his gardens—the wide beds along the front of the drive where the thick stands of iris, foxglove, and hollyhock thrived, or along the stone wall in back, weeding the peonies, or clipping the hedge, small bits of evergreen needles stuck to his sweaty chest. Mansfield and Daddy Harry would have men's days— where they would go off for full days into the woods with hatchet and chain saw. No amount of begging would open the way for a girl to join them. They would arrive home late, sweaty and covered in bark and dust. Only Mansfield was allowed into the sanctuary of our grandfather's bedroom. From the door where I hovered I could see hand-grips, rubber stretching devices, various weights—the paraphernalia of the culture of men's physical excellence. But it was always clear I was not welcome there, as if there was an invisible force field that rejected me.

One day when I was 12, I chanced upon a conversation where I was surprised to overhear Mansfield defending me. I had run along the flagstone walk, past the weathered white canvas chairs, up to the screen door of the summer section of The Farm. I was about to burst through in the usual way when something made me know to be quiet. I opened the screen door, holding the spring to silence its wrenching sound. Inside the hallway was cool, the two leather side chairs ringed in hammered brass fittings like sentinels at the foot of the stair. I heard voices and realized Mansfield and Daddy Harry were deep in conversation just around the corner in the sitting room. I sidled along the hall up to the doorway to listen, intrigued by an adult tone of seriousness. Daddy Harry said, "Why do you want to play w i t h her? She's just a girl." Then I heard Mansfield counter, "She's cool. If she wasn't my sister, I'd fuck her." All at once I was stung by my grandfather's easy and sweeping dismissal of me, but even more shocked that Mansfield dared to say fuck to him. I was cheered that my brother had stood up to him and come to my defense, in wonder that he dared offer a differing opinion. Even so I wanted to laugh at the swagger he'd tried to interject to burnish his nascent 14-year-old sexual bravado. The fact that he would have tried to fuck anything he could get his hands on at the time, which, since he confided in me, I knew to be nothing, was understood but not mentioned. Daddy Harry had the indulgence not to point this out, and the conversation turned to other things. I tiptoed backward and crept unheard up the stair, two steps at a time, to nurse this particular revelation in private. When Daddy Harry died more than a decade later, Mansfield sent this lone phrase, "He lives in me!" by letter back to our mother.

As an adult, Mansfield was known for preferring nudity and would usually answer his door naked. People took pictures of him doing so. He would dance around in the nude doing yoga postures and chanting Tibetan mantras. Back in the Surrey Street days, during the regular jam sessions into the night in his house, Mansfield would often play in the nude. Many years later, after he had moved to Mill Valley, his old friend Jeff, part of the family from those days, was visiting from LA with his wife. Remembering Mansfield's proclivities, Jeff arrived armed with a folded newspaper. When Mansfield opened the door in his usual way, Jeff quickly flourished the paper, holding it securely in front of Mansfield's genitals, shielding his wife's presumably delicate eyes and allowing her to enter unscathed by the rude shock of having to view Mansfield's dangling manhood up close.

Still, on good days now, Mansfield gives the impression of standing taller than himself, as though barely containing the sheer pleasure of his own physicality. There is a dignity and a prowess in this presence. Meeting neighbors in a brief exchange, it is as though his regard elevates the object of his attention and makes more vivid their own experience. Standing by his side, I feel the power of his containment conferred on me by proximity—it is as though the exuberance of his presence brings you viscerally into unwitting complicity with him. I've seen him have this effect on male clerks in CVS. It is an ability to create an intimate regard suffused with respect and this quality of laughing at the absurdity of life together. It is just Mansfield, playing, but it feels like a kind of love. After his death, a close friend of his, upon meeting me, said, "You know, your brother was extremely charismatic." She finished the sentence by looking at me doubtfully as if suspecting the person she saw in front of her couldn't possibly begin to comprehend the reality of what she meant.

Master Craftsman

To support his artwork, as the financial equation of life in San Francisco began to change, Mansfield started painting the San Francisco painted ladies, those ornamented crenellated Victorian houses whose architectural detailings are lovingly punctuated by gradations and contrasts of color. At first, he worked crews with his friends learning the trade and reported rollicking adventures. Sometime later, I recounted to him my outrage at a boyfriend who worked in film and photography, likely made more money than I did, and, through a personal contact at the IRS, was able to clean up 10 years of back taxes for less money than I paid in taxes in a single year. I was apoplectic that he enjoyed the financial freedom all that time, then was rewarded for it while I was the workaday drone paying my taxes like a chump. I noticed Mansfield was suddenly acutely interested, asking me about numbers and the time period forgiven. I realized he was calculating what it might take to undertake his own financial reckoning, to relegate his '60s ways to the past and enter a new freedom of legitimate standing in the world. Soon enough, likely motivated in part by his new fatherhood, he paid his back taxes, got his contractor's license, and began his own business. He ran large crews inside and out and would work those 12- or 14-hour days, often 7 days a week, for months at a time to support his months off making art or writing. The work drew on his penchant for discipline, precise technique and his appreciation for aesthetics. He was an exacting, master craftsman, consulted with colorists, knew gold-leaf and faux finishing techniques, and was quoted in local articles about the art and craft of restoration. When a big job was done, he would use those months off to do artwork or write at the same intensity. He had a job in the Castro district during one of those lovely breaks in the San Francisco weather when the fog lifted, and the sun shone for days on end. He and his crew stripped down and bent to their work. Weeks later, a friend handed him the area gay newspaper saying, "Check this out!" Front page center was a picture of Mansfield bare-backed, up on the scaffolding over the title "Hunk Of The Month." He relished the absurdity of it and laughed his high crowing laugh in the telling.

Luncheon
At The Farm—1960

O nce, at The Farm, Damma, our grandmother, decided to have a formal sit-down luncheon for a bevy of her closest 70-year-old friends. Mansfield volunteered to be head butler and volunteered me to be his assistant. We rehearsed various entries, protocols and signals between us. We polished the silverware, set the table with multiple forks and spoons, all the glass salt boats with their tiny ivory spoons, and the silver salt and pepper sets. We picked fresh flowers from Daddy Harry's garden and arranged them carefully on prongs in glass vases. When the guests came, Mansfield took on a grand swagger addressing each person as if she were a queen whose every need he was there to anticipate and satisfy. This pleased the ladies immensely and they were won over completely. We would be huddled in the kitchen and hear the rude rasping sound of Damma's nervous foot-buzzer secretly placed beneath the rug at her foot. This would signal a change in course and my brother would throw the butler's towel over his arm with panache and, head held at a commanding angle, burst through the swinging doors of the pantry into the dining room. Once there he became the consummate charmer while ordering me to hustle and do the dirty work. The luncheon was declared a great success, though we were never invited for a repeat performance.

When Mansfield was 12, there were serious behind-closed-doors conversations between him and our mother. This was unusual, and David and I watched with nervous alarm and an overriding curiosity. Mansfield had undertaken to read *The Rise and Fall of the Third Reich*. In the process, he'd developed a deep fascination, almost reverence, for Hitler. The response was swift and marked the ushering-in of a more solemn adult status—of accountability and consequences—that was foreign to our experience. Fortunately, this 12-year-old preoccupation was short-lived.

When he went away to Putney School, we all went on the drive down there. It was a mere hour away but felt like a major excursion into uncharted territory. We stopped first in Hanover at the Dartmouth Bookstore. Years later, he told me that he always thought of me as generous because that day I dipped into my saved allowance money and bought him a glossy book on sports cars that he suddenly coveted. My mother told me I was so distressed by his leaving that I had the hiccups the entire trip. I remember with envy seeing the hive of activity, his amazing modern dorm pod, and a small informal performance three upper classmen gave, playing guitars and singing. It was a simple ballad with a haunting melody that I remember to this day.

Within a few years, Mansfield's summer bedroom at The Farm was transformed into a sultan's lair. Walls and ceiling were hung with billowing Indian print bedspreads so no recognizable surface remained but the windows. Artwork was taped or pinned to the bedspreads and the only light allowed was red. At night the red light seemed to pulse and it was an inviting and clandestine place to be, as if you had crept inside someone's body. In daylight, it looked extreme, but not decadent. He got away with it because our grandparents rarely ventured above the first floor. He had an old suitcase record player and we listened to early Rolling Stones, Dylan, The Supremes. An ashtray with forbidden cigarette butts sat in the crook of the ledge, just outside the window but unobservable from below.

JOURNAL

Vette

March 13, 2001

Mansfield and I go to Office Max in San Rafael to pick up paper and ink cartridges. The place is a cavernous ghost town at mid-morning. We wait an interminable time while someone checks on something for us. I find myself becoming irrationally angry, as if I want to stamp my foot and blurt out, "Don't you realize you have a dying man here? He is too frail to be kept standing!" However, when we leave the store, Mansfield directs me to drive around the corner and park along a narrow access road. It appears he has more energy than I think. We walk back until we are eye-to-eye with a white Corvette nestled in amongst the other used cars in a small lot. "This is the one I want," he says. As he gazes at it, I can feel all that it means to him: power, lean bitchin' elegance, sculpted lines, speed, freedom, escape. He once told me he had always felt thwarted by his strongest appetites starting from when he was a small child and our family had been invited to a formal dinner party. A platter of food was passed among the children and Mansfield became transfixed by the ornate centerpiece made of foodstuff garnished with small flowers. He pointed to it and the host, with a wink at our mother, gave it to him on his own plate. He then had the object of his desire in front of him and so felt obliged to eat it. He did so and on the long drive home was violently sick and decidedly remorseful. He considered this an early lesson in a life-long theme about appetite that had often played itself out with vehicles. He gazed at the Corvette a long time. "I've always wanted one of these," he says. "A completely ridiculous and useless muscle car. At first I thought the car was gone," he muses, "I'm actually surprised it's still here." This is apparently his third visit to the car over the last few months while it sat beneath the late winter rains. "If I sold my truck, I could buy it outright," he says. His truck is gathering dust in the carport; I have been banned from driving it. He turns it over occasionally, to keep it alive, but his driving has been reduced to a small loop around the complex and once, a slow drive down to the farm at the head of Tennessee Valley Road, done only because he insisted and would not be opposed. We don't talk about that. Instead, he busies himself with mental calculations as to the likely price the truck would go for, subtracting out the price of the 'Vette, taxes, insurance. "I'll go talk to the guy," he says. I follow him into the office and stand at the back as they discuss the price and why the vehicle hasn't moved.

Impossibly, I want every one of his desires to be fully satisfied—especially this most absurd one. As if his wanting, the more outlandish the better, is a manifestation of the potent vein of life within him, a sign he is still amongst us. I wonder what the burly man behind the desk thinks of him—so thin he looks wraithlike and fragile with his bald head pale and oversized. But this is man talk and I hang back.

Later, Bill calls, his venture capital friend. "Is there anything he needs?" he asks. I have never met Bill, only heard his name, and never talked with him before. I cannot think on my feet. Later, I kick myself for not saying "Can you please get him a drive in a white 'Vette? He just wants to head north on 101 and keep going."

Truck

March 15, 2001

We go out and sit in the truck. He wants to keep the engine alive, so we just sit there while he revs it. He tells me about the time, before his meds were regular, when he went out to turn over the truck and could not figure out how to get the key in the door. Nor could he fathom how to get mail out of his mailbox, something he tried to do on the same excursion. I shudder at this image of his flailing vulnerability. I am concerned, idling in the parking bay beneath his apartment, that the exhaust fumes will snake up and in the window polluting the air we will soon breathe when we go back inside. I find myself reasoning that he doesn't need airborne chemicals in his compromised system, as if whether he is subject to them or not will make a difference now in the trajectory of his illness. Despite my irritating worrywart proclivities, I manage to let go of this apprehension, and keep my mouth shut. He releases the brake, and the truck rolls out lazily onto the blacktop. He takes it up the hill to the top end of the other side of the complex as though there is pleasure in the simple competence of driving: pressing the clutch, moving into gear and easing the truck along. I know this feeling. Despite my periodic panic attacks on the road, I have another side of me that loves to drive my friend Tony's Porsche, letting it out to 120 miles per hour on the open road in Maine, for which I am banned from driving in Maine for two months. At the top of the hill, Mansfield sees his friend Gary. He pulls over and they jam—a casual male-to-male bravado. Gary says, "Good to see you out."

I know that when I've been away Mansfield has taken the truck along the winding Tennessee Valley Road, one of his favorite places. It alarms and scares me, given how often I've seen him nod out. But I admire his sneaking around me, just doing what he wants. I feel my own desperation in my desire for control, like maybe if I can control enough, he won't have to die. I can feel it annoys him and he just needs to break my shackles by doing something himself, on his own time. I can't imagine giving up driving. There is something unholy in wanting to impose that restriction on someone else, for whatever seemingly good reason, as if it were a kind of neutering, a power play forcing an adult back into the dependency of a child. It is yet another insult, a death before death. I know once he's even driven with Paul to San Rafael. "You know I wouldn't let him do it if it wasn't safe," he had assured me.

Lightnin'

March 16, 2001

Lightnin' lives across the bridge in Pacific Heights with his wife, Tokey and The Boy. He is a stalwart supporter of Mansfield, arriving regularly after work in the early evening for two-hour stints when Mansfield could not be left alone. Even since I've come, he continues to come to spell me periodically, giving me a chance to run off into town and do whatever I feel like doing. I treasure this, even if it is to only walk around the center of Mill Valley, staring into store windows or perusing a wall of books at the Depot Café. Lightnin' sits with his arms crossed, a pillar of patience and devoted service, while Mansfield sleeps. He is practical—he thinks to take care of Mansfield's truck when it dies and needs a jump, when the registration needs renewing. Lightnin' is a regular fixture in the rhythm of Mansfield's life, but I have not gotten to know him well, since I am always leaving as soon as he arrives, hurrying to make use of the time he has given me. He is quiet, a soft-spoken man of few words. He is a scientist by training, a biologist with an abiding commitment to the notion of sustainability. I heard from Mansfield that, back in the late '60s days of pot, acid and limitless midnight munchies, he'd earned the name Lightnin' by being Magnolia Thunderpussy's fastest delivery boy, ferrying erotic designer sundaes to the city's late night hipsters and visiting musicians. I never met The Boy, but I know he was the beneficiary of Mansfield's sax, which would not have been bestowed lightly.

Today I finally connect with Bob, whose party Marie and I went to my first week here. I am able to retrieve my shoes and return the shoes I inadvertently walked off in that night. My shoes are now stretched bigger than they should be.

Loveland Road

Toward the end of grade school we lived at the top of Loveland Road, in Norwich, Vermont, a curvy, pocked, dirt ascent that ended at our house. Mansfield one day decided he would change our customary way of walking home from where the school bus dropped us at the bottom of the hill, on Route 5. Where it had always been him first, me lagging somewhat behind, and our younger brother David straggling along still further behind, this day he refused to let me go second. He instead pushed my younger brother ahead of me and consistently blocked my passage at every move, egging David on to stay ahead of me. Finally, in a spasm of fury, I stalked off into the woods. I found a rotten log and sat there in a steaming, and then bored and scratchy, silence. I was enraged that he had exerted power over me and upended my rightful place. When I strode into dinner three hours later, nothing was said. He had made his point—that he was stronger than I. I had made mine—he never did it again. Of course, he didn't have to.

Ross

March 19, 2001

Mansfield is getting more adventurous: there is a new place he wants to hike. We drive north on 101 and head west on Sir Frances Drake Highway toward Ross. He directs me, after a few exploratory wrong turns, to park along the edge of the street in a rural, sparsely populated neighborhood. We walk down to where he thinks the trail begins. He descends the ditch in order to scale a small embankment to get to the trail. He miscalculates his strength. His footing gives way and he falls to his knees, clawing at grasses and branches to keep himself from slipping back. I hold my breath at the spectacle of his frailty, his body collapsed like a praying mantis, the cords of his neck straining to hold up his bald head. Sheer will propels him forward, and he has to rest, gasping for breath, at the crest of the small rise he would easily have taken in a single leap, before. I feel I have to look away, allowing him privacy as he registers how far he has fallen from his old prowess. We muster ourselves and continue at a slow amble. The path is clear and shaded and gradual and leads us to a small clearing with a bench and a view. We sit to rest. In moments, he turns and lies back along the bench until his head rests in my lap, his eyes gazing at the sky—an inconceivable intimacy before his illness.

Jack

March 20, 2001

When I first take a call from Jack, I don't know the voice and ask who it is. He states, "John Miller," in the deepest voice, so stentorian and officious it scares me, as though he were the debt collector for the Bardo. I quickly hand the phone to Mansfield and moments later hear a peal of laughter and, "Jack!" They can rave for hours, and do, both being generators and storytellers with a strong predilection for philosophical speculation and 30 years of shared experience to draw on. Mansfield reveres Jack for his intelligence, erudition, commanding ability to conceptualize and articulate, and his serious-ness as a poet. Jack admires Mansfield's discipline and seriousness as an artist. They know each other's foibles like their own.

When Jack calls and Mansfield is asleep, I settle in for some demanding entertainment. He once told me, and then demonstrated, how he fooled one of his broth-ers who runs a museum in New Orleans, by posing as a major potential donor. He disguised his voice, took on a complex persona, and over a number of months led his brother to believe the museum was about to be the recipient of a considerable capital bequest. He played both parts to me—the measured professionalism of his brother, the easy drawl and minutely irritating concerns of the donor. He was so convincing it was breathtaking. We roared with laughter. "Yeah ... he was kind of upset when he found out it was me," he admitted sheepishly. "I think he didn't talk to me for awhile ... at least a couple of months."

Jack is down in McAllen, Texas, where he has gone to attend to his aging parents. His wife left him, his mother has since died, and his dear friend Mansfield is dying. He is Director of the McAllen International Museum of Arts and Sciences, and he and Mansfield have contrived a plan to give 35 of Mansfield's art pieces to the Museum. They joke that McAllen will host Mansfield's first major show—posthumously—in about 8 months.

I have an image of Jack standing just outside his house, having navigated corridors of boxes he has yet to unpack from the move from San Francisco two years earlier, in order to grab a smoke while observing the pelting rain that creates steam and no relief from the heat save the spectacle of a million tiny frogs unleashed on the land by some fecund alchemy. He bemusedly reports all this over the long-distance static of the storm and gripes, "I'm a poet! I don't know if I can do one more gala event. I'm great on TV, talking up the Museum, the kids' program, our new addition. And the ladies love me at cocktail parties, if I do say so. But I miss my own work. I'm not cut out to do this 80 hours a week. I yearn to go be in a cabin on the edge of the high desert." I hear his deep growly voice and my own soft liquid sound and, in the free play that distance allows it feels like the essence of male and female entwining on the edge of the abyss. "Death is so erotic," I say. "Yes, Sweet," he says. "It is. Terribly so."

Memories of early
days in Vermont

March 22, 2001

Cards again. It must remind Mansfield of The Farm too because he tells me a story of that late summer in 1958. He was nine and I was seven and we were living at The Farm for summer vacation, we had been told. Our mother invited Mansfield to go for a ride. He said he felt like a big shot because it was just the two of them, David and I being left at home. They drove from Windsor to Norwich, and somewhere along the beautiful and winding Route 5 she told him that she and Dad would not be living together anymore. He couldn't comprehend what it meant. "You mean I'll live with Dad and David and Anne will live with you?" he asked. "No," she said. "It means you will all three live with me and we will not be going back to Michigan." They got to the Colt House, where she said we would soon be living, and he could only wander around in a daze, unable to take in anything. When they got back home to The Farm, he ran up to his room. He gathered all his money, $2.87, and took it to her. He said, "Here. If I give you all the money I have, can I go live with Dad?" She said, "No, it doesn't work that way."

Later she suggested he write a letter to Dad. He did. He wrote: "I know you and Mom hate each other, but you're the best Dad in the world." He put the letter in an envelope, snuck downstairs, and ran through the yard to the mailbox behind the hedge at the end of the driveway and stuck the letter inside. Back upstairs, he watched

Mom go to the mailbox and get his letter. She came back and said to him, "It's not like that. We don't hate each other. It's just not good for us to live together anymore." Another incomprehensible statement that he'd carried intact over 43 years of living to tell me over a card game.

Though we were a blaring anomaly—the only family in our new world who were divorced as far as we knew—the Colt House had its consolations. Standing in a row of houses along the perimeter of Main Street and the Norwich Green, which doubled as a schoolyard, it was one of four imposing houses (three brick and one clapboard) originally owned by the family that made the Colt 45 pistol. We thought this noteworthy in itself. In the fourth house down, the lone clapboard one hiding behind a thicket of trees, lived an old lady who made dolls with the perfect likeness of their prospective young owners. This struck us as magical and somehow sinister. In our house, the front entrance, rarely used, had two curving staircases that made a graceful arc and met at the second floor. On the roof was a widow's walk, though there was no ocean in sight. Out back was a sunken garden, allowed to go to riot within the angular brick walls, filled with peonies and great yellow and black-spotted spiders. Between the garden and house was a small apple orchard. Every room had its own fireplace. Out the window of the middle bedroom was a grape vine trained to grow up the lattice, hanging its clusters within reach—though we had to wait a long time before they became sweet. The best room had built-in bookshelves, so that every inch of wall space could be used to put stuff in.

It would get very cold at night, and in the morning the floorboards would be freezing underfoot, making it hard to get out of bed. Once Mansfield woke me in the middle of the night and we crept downstairs. Out the kitchen windows a low fog hung beneath the apple trees, and he showed me deer moving in shadowy congregation, eating the sweet fallen apples from the ground. We stared out into the darkness for a while, then he climbed up on the counter to reach the cookie jar high up on the shelf and we had an illicit feast.

A low white stable-like structure with green, arced openings ran at right angles to the rear of the house. Soon after we moved there, Mansfield explored the cobwebby attic that ran the length of it. He found sheaves of drawings of buildings, page after page rendered with loving accuracy. He was thrilled with his find —the precision and ambition of it—and it was the beginning of his passion for making visual things.

Soon after we moved into the Colt House, I entered the third grade. One day, I found no one home after school. I heard noises in the basement and then a stranger emerged. It was someone disguised as my mother with uncanny accuracy, but who was revealed as a fake because certain details were just not right. The eyebrows were too dark, as if painted on. The eyelids finely rimmed in black, lurid, as though someone dark and diabolical had wanted to look just like my mother. This person stood looking at me. In horror, I backed away. In a terror-stricken instant, I knew the world as fundamentally unsafe. My father had been taken away, and now, suddenly, my mother had also gone, and in her place was this malign imposter. I knew my brothers were still with me. They had been at school and just weren't home yet. I still had allies. This person in front of me laughed, suspiciously trying to set me at ease. She went into the big kitchen and stood at the sink, running water over her face. "See.... the soot's all gone," she said, drying her face and looking up. "The furnace blew up!" She laughed. I stood watching her, wanting to believe, but the shock had registered and a part of me was held separate.

Dr. Pond

March 22, 2001

Dr. Pond seems like a mythical figure. Mansfield always speaks with reverence of his excellence as a physician, his command of an impossibly busy practice and the fact that he is a serious cellist. All big decisions that Margaret makes are corroborated with Pond. He is the unseen team member presiding over Mansfield's life from afar. When we are told he will come for a visit, there is a flurry of excitement and anticipation—as far as that is possible for someone whose life is mostly sleep. We vacuum and make more order than we usually demand of ourselves. We wait as dusk descends over the Marin hills.

Finally, he comes, a neat compact man, sure and precise in his movements. "I got lost," he says. "Oh, I probably gave you the wrong address," says Emma easily, "I'm always mixing up the numbers." "You must be the daughter I've heard about," he says, warmly. Mansfield sits poised and contained on his mattress in the middle of the room, amid his mountain of pillows. He introduces me, and then he greets Dr. Pond with affection and respect.

Dr. Pond sits down on the mattress next to him. "You're a little low on furniture, aren't you Mansfield?" he says. Mansfield, in all his dignity, says nothing, while I say, "He's given it all away in his various purges." This is true, but I felt a poor spiritedness in my comment and regret the shame it exhibits. I want to protect and excuse my brother's ways when, in fact, his own integrity and dignity are intact. My comment goes unacknowledged, which only embarrasses me further.

The conversation continues with Dr. Pond asking Emma about her life at the University of Chicago and then asking Mansfield about how he has been feeling. Eventually, Mansfield maneuvers the conversation around to dying and the fact that he'd rather go sooner than have to await the incremental breakdown and disintegration of his body. He lists the various alternatives he's looked into and the particular problems associated with each. Dr. Pond has undoubtedly heard much of this before, but he listens respectfully and, when Mansfield is done, reminds him of the law. Later, after Pond is gone, Mansfield says, "I think he heard me," with a knowing wink.

My Pops

March 24, 2001

Emma is at the University of Chicago and has lived with Mansfield's illness for three and a half of her four years there. This means that when he is well, they might go to Hawaii on vacation. When he is not, she stays at his bedside while her friends are out and about. He worships her openly, marveling how a creature of such womanly beauty could have sprung from him. They have a lively intellectual partnership going back to her childhood, which continues in weekly extended Saturday morning telephone calls while she is at university. They debate the issues in her courses and argue the fine points of intellectual or philosophical distinctions. He once crowed with delight and pride when she received an A on a paper she'd rewritten after they'd revisited her original premise and crafted a new line of thought. When she showed interest in film he worried over her choice of an artistic career, not wanting for her the suffering he had endured. Sometimes, after encounters with her friends' families he would admit humiliation. "I'm just a housepainter," he'd say, reducing himself to that single word, implying that those families' prosperity put his own failings in high relief.

When Emma was much younger, they would go to the Devil's Slide and spend hours cavorting on the beach. During one of my visits, the three of us went to Japantown and saw warrior movies, so eye-poppingly brutal that I had to pretend they were comic books. When I looked over at Emma, I realized she was a seasoned viewer, her small serious face evaluating the skill with which the makeup people had embedded the hatchet so realistically in the center of the antagonist's skull. On another visit, Mansfield toured us around in a red muscle car he'd bought that had leopard skin seats. As Emma approached adolescence, he reported his heartbreak that her thoughts were turning elsewhere—she no longer took the same unalloyed delight in their encounters as did he.

Now, her spring break is coming to a close. She says, "I just want to be with my Pops." As I leave the room, she slides into bed and lies against his back with her arms around him. Later, after she left, he told me he'd turned his face to the wall and wept for her sweetness and the intensity of his love for her.

Rent

March 30, 2001

"**I**'m going to pay the rent," Mansfield says, pulling on his pants and a sweatshirt.

"I'll come see where you do that," I say, not saying that I may soon have to do it by myself.
We stroll to the bottom of the hill.

"No one home," he notes, seeing the car gone. He drops the envelope in the mail slot and we turn to go back up the hill.

"I want them to see me looking healthy—I'm afraid if they know I'm dying, they will throw me out," he says matter-of-factly.

I am pierced by his feeling of vulnerability, by the fact that he carries not only the daily evidence of his own physical decline, but an underlying fear he will suffer punishment for it too. We continue walking in silence as I grope for a response.

Then he asks, casually, "How long do you think you'll be here?" I am surprised that he even has the question. Yet it mirrors my own internal conversations, where I find myself noting his improving energy levels and immediately mentally extend my stay accordingly. It is an odd juxtaposition—delight and celebration at each increment of returning vitality and a corresponding moment-by-moment calculus about what it means for me. I feel incapable of talking about it openly. Even now, I search for words carefully. I don't say, "Until you die," as if wanting at some level to preserve whatever hope might be operant inside him. Instead, I say, "I will be here as long as you want me to." I feel his body ease, get the palpable sense that he allows himself to relax into knowing he is held and exempt from having to find another solution to his increasingly dependent state. There will be no banishment.

Gas station, Miller Avenue

April 2, 2001

Monthly, I go into the gas station on the south side of Miller Avenue, where I rent my car. After I arrived, Mansfield decided his truck was unreliable, and particularly unsuitable if I drive to see my friend in Vallejo. So, I rented, not thinking much of it, and the time that at first seemed it would be weeks turned into months. The Asian owner or his wife or son always preside from behind the counter over a continuous flurry of activity. I wait my turn, reading the testimonials and studying the cluster of photographs of local people who love this place. There is a letter from Peter Coyote, wedding pictures, family outings, baby pictures. When I get to the counter, the owner pulls me up on the screen.

"You rent too much! You should buy car!" he exclaims.

"Oh!" I say, surprised. I rush to say, "But I don't live here. I take care of Mansfield, my brother, who is so sick. He's your customer; he sent me here."

"Ohhhh...tsk, tsk," he says. "You wait." He rushes out and comes back a moment later with a shock of heather, lilies and roses that he lays across my arms. He goes behind the counter again. "We get you best price, best price!" he says.

I stand at the counter with my arms full of flowers and weep.

Illness

The first time Mansfield got sick, six years before, he thought he had an extreme case of food poisoning. His friends Paul and Tereza were already headed south on a weekend jaunt out of the city when they spontaneously decided they'd go check in on Mansfield, having not seen him in a while. They turned around and headed up to Mill Valley, where they found him weak, trembling, blue-lipped, saying he'd eaten something that didn't agree with him. Tereza, with a nurse's eye, declared that it was not food poisoning and insisted he go to a hospital. Even in his weakened state, he stubbornly resisted her. She was able to prevail, and he soon enough learned he had an obscure form of cancer of the jujeunum that manifested as an obstruction in the middle of his small intestine. As he told me this, shortly after, when his prognosis was still uncertain, I knew he would be OK, and, as it turned out, he was. They removed a large tumor and, after some time, declared him cancer-free. He remarked how delighted he was to have had a female surgeon, a sure sign of his recovery.

In late 1997, though, the message was different. I picked up the phone one cold November night, on my way out the door to meet my new West Coast swing dance partner at the old VFW hall in Cambridge. Mansfield's voice was feeble, without its rich resonance. It sounded thin, airy, insubstantial, as though he could not get a purchase on anything solid and had to accept defeat. I could not argue with that. I could look for ways around the diagnosis, but the timbre of his voice pierced me with a knowing I could not deny. It narrowed my attention immediately. "They give me about a year," he said. "I've started to clear things out: books, sculptures, furniture." He continued his litany as though focusing on the pragmatic would mitigate the wild grief that rose up inside me, the rage so overwhelming it wanted to slip into denial.

It was a brief call, because I had no way to reach my dance partner, who would have long since left his house. I went blindly to the VFW hall. In my ringing shock I felt as though I inhabited a bubble of absolute alarm. The sultry, smoky music came at me as though from a great distance. I found my friend in the crowd and spilled out "I just found out that my brother will die within a year," hoping he would tell me it wasn't so. He paused, looked down at the floor, thought for a moment and then said, "Sometimes, when you hear something like that, it can be good to just move your body."

I felt utterly without resources to deal with this. Instead of a place where I held death as a natural part of living, I experienced a dark lacuna ringed with blanching fear and, when that could no longer be borne, the numbness of denial. I'd had few experiences with death. Deaths in my childhood—an elderly babysitter, my great grandmother—were hushed events that occurred elsewhere. When our beloved collie was put to sleep, when I was still in grade school, we were told about it afterwards, as if the messiness of our feelings about it couldn't be managed, and therefore had to be nipped in the bud. I found out my grandfather had died by sheer chance when I happened to drive through Hanover, New Hampshire, two and a half hours from where I lived at the time and spotted my mother's car incongruously parked in town in the middle of the morning. I instantly knew he had died, and found her in the local coffee shop, sitting at the counter alone, nursing a coffee and cigarette with trembling hands, as she digested this new reality. Seven years later, I received a letter from her telling me that my grandmother had died. The letter arrived the day she was en route to the funeral, in another state, precluding any possibility of my participating in the event. Whether this was because she thought only of herself, didn't think I would be interested or that my busy life wouldn't allow me the time to accompany her was a matter of conjecture. In the time before cell phones, it was a moot point.

Mansfield had survived his earlier diagnosis of cancer. My mother had first been diagnosed with cancer when I was in my late twenties, and was told she had two years to live, but she outfoxed death and lived another eighteen years. My joke was that the doctor hadn't taken into account how practiced she was at pickling herself in alcohol. By that time, I had come to recognize that her relationship with alcohol was not the norm and had implications for me.

I had visited my uncle's girlfriend, Evelyn, shortly before her death. As we laughed and told stories, comparing notes on the history of alcohol in our respective families, she wanted to demonstrate what beautiful legs she had had in her early drinking and dancing days. She pulled her leg from beneath the covers, angling it up toward the ceiling as if it were in a high heel. Admiring her still beautiful curves I was overcome with sorrow and wept openly. As I sat by her side trying to contain myself, I noticed a soft breeze coming in through the window on the other side of her bed. Something in that awareness told me that everything was exactly as it was supposed to be. I felt a kind of wonder, but the information was unmistakable: this dying was unfolding perfectly.

Another time, a woman I had known as part of an Adult Children of Alcoholics therapy group was hospitalized with end stage cancer. She requested that a number of us visit her, and we were arrayed around her bed, chatting. A nurse whisked in and reminded her it was time for her catheterization. She said to just go ahead with it, and we all looked on as the nurse quickly pulled back the sheet and peeled away the labial folds to insert the catheter. There was a shock of sudden inadvertent voyeurism, of witnessing the site of intimacy treated with a matter-of-factness befitting the absurd mechanics of being physical. Shortly after, as we were preparing to leave, our friend invited us all to come visit her on the North Shore where she could host us properly, when she felt better. Seeing the power of her desire to cling to her beloved everyday—her place overlooking the river, tea with friends—to the point that she would beg us to collude in her hope, broke me open. By the time I made it out of the hospital, I was sobbing. When my wave of grief subsided, everything around me was starkly alive: the lined pavement before me animated by a million tiny flecks of mica in the white lines, the poppy red of the flowers across the way, a shimmering quality of light in the air, as if everything was freshly washed and more vividly itself than ever.

None of these experiences, intense as each one was, prepared me for Mansfield's dying. I was as raw and prone to denial as ever. Mansfield instinctively knew to mitigate this by focusing on facts. He was diagnosed with leiomyosarcoma. When he first told me, his tongue wrapped around the word, caressing it as if he were savoring an exotic fruit. He spelled it for me. He was exploring it, educating himself, coming to terms, informing the multitude of his extended family.

Leiomyosarcoma is a rare form of cancer that forms in the soft tissue cells of smooth, involuntary muscles, which means it can start anywhere in the body there is a blood vessel. It can stay in one place, quiet for 20 years; it can spread wildly all over the body; or it can do one and then the other on no specific timetable. It is not particularly responsive to chemo or radiation and so is best treated by surgical removal with a wide margin around the tumor while it is still small, before it spreads. Late diagnosis is common, however, due to an absence of symptoms. It is resistant, aggressive, unpredictable and rare. Sarcomas are just 1% of all cancers; of the 70 or so soft tissue sarcomas, Leiomyosarcoma is one of the more common, accounting for 25% of all newly diagnosed soft tissue sarcomas. Causes are not well understood, though genetic risk factors and exposure to high radiation or certain chemicals are thought to possibly play a part. Medical opinions change from month to month, both on diagnosis and on some aspects of treatment. Recently, newer more targeted therapies have come available using drugs or manmade versions of immune system antibodies to block cancer cell growth while leaving normal cells untouched.

Mansfield placed himself fully in Dr. Pond's care. But early on, his enterprising spirit took the lead in investigating a parallel course of multiple alternative treatments, which he could enter into while awaiting the scheduling of his medical procedures. He investigated a heat cure, but discovered it not recommended for the profile of his cancer. He played with a laughter cure, going through *L'il Abner* and other comics that would touch him off. He tried a garlic cure, where he ate large quantities of raw garlic for extended periods of time until he claimed people could tell he was present by the smell, before he even entered a room. He investigated Philippine spiritual healers who were said to be able to pluck illnesses from the body and he researched other shamanic healers people told him about. Later, he investigated the Hemlock Society, schooling himself in the possibilities of committing suicide. He looked into the parameters of being eligible for physician-assisted suicide either in Oregon or The Netherlands. Cruelly, whenever Mansfield was most inclined to take this route, he found himself too ill to travel, or he learned that some detail of the formal requirements for eligibility ruled him out. At every turn he felt thwarted in his desire to be able to die with dignity. He had been robustly physical and healthy, and contemplating a slow inexorable loss of his physical life was anathema to him.

When Mansfield first received the leiomyosarcoma diagnosis, he was told he likely had a year to live. As he contemplated the grueling 3 days of 5-hour chemo treatments every 3 weeks, he said he would prefer to go in three months. When that didn't happen, over time he became more resigned, philosophical.

"At every stage I've said, 'Ah hah!'" he told me, "as though I always knew it would be thus. I do believe you have little mind and great mind, the collective unconscious. Everything is known". He described a war zone atmosphere when four doctors congregated after an early treatment. One young doctor suggested they could assess whether Mansfield had turned a corner when he came back in six months. Later, an older one said, "Don't be naïve!" and read him the riot act. "He had a rough bedside manner," Mansfield noted. Dr. Pond said, more skillfully: If necessary, they could go back in, in six months.

In one conversation Mansfield said, "My sadness is tremendous. I don't sob. Life is so delightful—it's a tragedy. Granny, Betty, Daddy Harry, Damma, Mom and Dad," he said, naming relatives in the order of their deaths. "It's harder to bear. Why me? You die alone. My strategy is to do all I can to create a psychological state I can endure. Resignation is where it's at. The inevitability of it."

Mansfield did not die in one year. Three weeks after one of the chemo rounds was completed, he complained, "I still almost never go out. I'm eating, able to be conscious. But people's careers intervene. 'Mansfield's dying' is old news now." He experienced prolonged lassitude. He described relief at discovering that dilaudid was much more tolerable than morphine for the pain he endured. He reported talking with his friend Paul in Australia, a bright spot. He said Lightnin' came across the bridge to spend time with him almost every other night, for which he was profoundly grateful. He reported that Emma was a first-rate caregiver: "She's very tolerant," he observed. A number of his CAT scans were "virtually identical," leaving him completely depressed and miserable. One cancer had been larger and was cleared up a bit, and elsewhere there were some new ones, as if everything were held in check. He described a thalidomide treatment designed to shrink the production of tiny new blood vessels around the cancers in an attempt to keep it from going hog wild. "The fact of my death I've come to accept. What troubles me is my mind," he mused. Then, "I don't want to die. But, if I don't die, I will probably step on a tack and then die of the ketuzelums." He was quoting our grandfather, a small sign his humor was coming back.

Family Reunion

March 1999

Not long after his doctors announced a new timetable for his dying, Mansfield called for a family gathering, saying we should come soon. We congregated at the Holiday Inn near the Dipsea Restaurant, not far from where he lived. I arrived first in the benign night air, which smelled remarkably of fresh earth and flowering plants in early March. Soon, my younger sister Robin arrived with her husband Joel and young Fletcher and Lyle in tow. Though Robin was sired by a different father, after Mansfield had left home for high school, they had a special bond. Perhaps it was the understanding of two similar sensibilities, first and last born, having been tempered by the brunt of our mother's cyclonic energy. Robin's kids, at 1 and 3, were little generators, eager to find a new appreciator for their noisy enthusiasms. When my younger brother, David, arrived from Maine, his burly presence took top billing. We entered Robin's hotel room together, and the boys erupted with shouts of "DAVID!!" and rushed at him, clamoring to show him their toys. Finally, our father came in from Michigan, dapper in slacks, sweater vest, jacket, trench coat and hat, bringing the formality of another era. He had an uncertain air, polite and courtly. He was gentlemanly to Robin, whom he had last seen as a young child, and to her family, whom he had never met. He rubbed his hands together in the anticipatory pleasure of having us all together for, remarkably, the first time since we were teenagers. Yet, he seemed tentative, almost apologetic, reminding me of the quiet undertow of sorrow: he was an 80-year-old man, entirely unprepared to see his oldest son dying at the age of 50.

Mansfield orchestrated us, meting out his time in increments so he could pace himself and marshal his energies. We were an onslaught, arriving at his place at the appointed mid-morning time. It was shocking to see his frailty, but there was a festive air brought on by the sheer numbers and variety of people sprawled in his living room. He had conscripted his West Coast family to help manage us. Jonathan, whom I'd met at least once before, came and herded us to the Depot Café for lunch. He attended to us all, solicitous in a special way to each—for example telling my diffident father hero stories about Mansfield. His intense presence and charm were disarming and helped us navigate the emotion of seeing Mansfield so diminished. Mansfield's vulnerability was more apparent outside: his uncharacteristically slow walking (he had taught me to speed-walk as a teenager), his head at times appearing almost skeletal, his usually robust body lost beneath the folds of excess fabric in his everyday pants, which hung from his hips, as though on a hanger with nothing inside.

Sitting outside at the Depot, something came up in my conversation with Mansfield that made me realize he had probably earned three or four times what I had supposed in his business. I was aware of him watching me work through the inner computations. He laughed as he witnessed my struggle to reconcile this with our running conversations about wealth, poverty and how to live with dignity. I saw he might be physically weakened, but was mentally sharp as ever, tracking my dawning comprehension with delight, relishing his setup. It reminded me of when I first heard him exclaim, "You must be a genius!" to someone else. I had assumed that when he said it to me, even if just having fun, he sort of meant it. I only realized my foolishness when he laughed at my private dismay, like it was a cosmic joke he had instigated for my rude but necessary awakening.

The next day, Susan, Emma's mother, and Jonathan joined us for a walk in the woods in Tennessee Valley. We were a sprawling congregation, the kids darting ahead, all of us pausing periodically to rest, sitting on the huge trunk of a fallen tree. Later, a smaller group of us made an excursion to Sausalito, pausing to sit and talk at various places along the waterfront. We gathered the next morning at the Dipsea Restaurant for a serious breakfast before leaving. I was surprised and touched to see that Jonathan had come again, all the way from the far side of the Bay Bridge in Emoryville, to see us off.

Dad

Late June, 2000

Mansfield listened acutely when I called from Flint, Michigan, where David and I huddled at the hospital. I described Dad's impossible condition, wavering in a coma as his organs shut down one by one. I described the shock of seeing the painful accumulation of water that made him blow up like a balloon, the fragile membrane of his pale skin terribly distended. I told him about the awkwardness of having to argue forcefully with Sue, Dad's wife, who, as his medical executor, needed convincing to authorize the doctors to turn off the life support, which was only keeping him in that horrifying suspension. His death signaled a dire turn in her own circumstances, bedridden as she was and entirely reliant on his support for her own quality of life. She teetered between insisting on the thread of a possibility of his life and accepting cataclysm into her own. Mansfield listened quietly, removed from the drama I was recounting. But I sensed there was a deep inner calculus underway in him, perhaps measuring the threshold our father faced, and appreciating Dad's wisdom in going before Mansfield himself did.

Later, we marveled and celebrated Dad's grace in dying so quickly, with no real decline, only a hovering, a mere three days between his burst aneurism—a condition that he'd carried around for years, like a fresh egg on a spoon he had to take care not to drop—and his death. There was some foreknowing there, as he suddenly got his financial papers signed the day before it happened, foregoing his usual Ruykeyser and *Washington Week* TV lineup to enlist a friend into sudden service to witness his signing. He drove on Saturday night to his favorite refuge, his small office away from home in the middle of a dry-cleaning plant he owned, where everything was within easy reach and there were secret places for private papers. He had the wherewithal to call each of us that night, a call I received only as a routine voicemail. In the middle of his conversation with my younger brother, David, his aneurysm burst. My brother quickly deduced this as my father was suddenly not present on the call but could be heard groaning on the floor. David called the County Sheriff and directed them to where he was. He was rushed to the hospital and apparently had a few amiable words with the EMTs because later, surprisingly, they showed up at his funeral, saying they had found him so charming. It was as though at some level, a decision had been made, a recognition that the time was upon him, and a simple execution of last things performed with no muss. I recalled asking him shortly after our mother died, whether he feared death. He paused a moment and said, "No," with a quiet finality that was like a closing door—no further conversation required. On our long drive back from his funeral in a U-Haul truck—where we'd packed a few keepsakes and his coveted woodworking tools a week later, on the night of July 4th, David and I watched a succession of fireworks periodically animate the night sky as we moved east from Michigan across Upstate New York, our own private silent fanfare.

I had reconnected with Dad when I was about 27, after a 10-year hiatus when the generational divide of the '60s played itself out in our particular family diaspora. I recall the unexpected delight in discovering, when I arrived at our cousins' cottage on the coast of Maine while Dad and his brother Buck were still out, that he had a large binder where he kept lists of new words he had heard, with dividers for sections where he recorded definitions, samples of how they might be used, and intriguing ideas that had come to him. Many years later, while cleaning out his house, I found the daily pocket version where these thoughts and words were first recorded, interspersed with shopping lists and reminders. He also loved car design, immediately recognizing the turn of a particular grill, the taper of a fin, the roll of a fender—perhaps Mansfield had inherited his appreciation for cars. Born of his childhood in the Depression, he had a keen nose for a deal. He went to Michigan car auctions until he'd land one he could really brag about, once an old silver-gray, chrome-roofed Cadillac Coupe de Ville, built as an experimental design model, which was a steal at the price he paid.

The same impulse toward frugality, we discovered when cleaning out his house, kept him filling bureau drawers until they were mausoleums of unopened Christmas presents from distant, dutiful children—sweaters, shirts, socks and wallets, all in their plastic wrappers—while he frequented the local thrift store for buys. Mansfield reported that they had numerous conversations that consisted entirely of joke telling, which would end only when they were both worn out, the upper registers of their voices stretched and tears in their eyes from laughing so hard. In a random conversation about the foibles of both of our parents, Mansfield had told me how he admired and emulated Dad's grace in interacting with other people, the unfailing respect and courteousness he emanated. Being more like him myself, I saw it as a little too heavy on the diffident, self-effacing side, though I did know one woman who claimed she and her mother always got along better when he came to visit. In a rare family reunion in Salt Lake City, I had witnessed my father deferring to his flamboyant older brother, Buck. At the time I had willed him to be more assertive, losing sight of the fact that we were in Buck's family's territory and they were merely playing out the dynamic of their parents, where mother Elsa was a center-stage partier and toward the end of her life, a serious drinker, while her husband was a quiet, unassuming engineer.

Big Al, as Dad was known to some, one year bought a new Honda CRX, because he so admired mine. Despite his loving its pep and handling, he could only own it for a few months before he had to sell it, the discomfort of having paid full price for a new vehicle so went against his sensibilities. He suffered intense shame when a dry-cleaning customer accused him of being cheap and stingy to the point of being unethical because of the financial offer he made to her for a damaged garment. He had no comprehension of the real current price of any piece of clothing because, on principle, he could never pay full price himself. This impossible double-bind led to a painful outbreak of shingles, a virus that may lie dormant in nerve tissues for decades and then be triggered by a stressful life event. His condition caused and was exacerbated by insomnia, and we all were the recipients of long wide-ranging letters, his way of navigating this protracted crisis.

In one of them, he told the story of his coming of age in the run up to Pearl Harbor and World War II. "To follow up on this colorless career of mine," he describes how a series of moves precipitated by a much older brother, and serendipity, kept him from being drafted into the infantry. He taught mechanics to civilian employees in one of the many air depots across the country. Asked to critique the training of civilians for airplane maintenance, he wrote a report suggesting that the prevailing practice was too generalized, that you couldn't equip people to know everything about an airplane. Training specific to electrical systems, engines or whatever other aspect, he suggested, would produce a cadre of people well prepared to service aircraft. "They read that letter and hired me on the spot. It's interesting what the effect of good writing can do. I sometimes see what I write and realize that it really sounds better than I am. That I'm not as smart as my writing may indicate." I recognized his self-deprecation as uncomfortably familiar, and also saw his reluctance to take credit for the value of his thinking, which was so clearly demonstrated in his story.

His shingles episode caused by shame echoed the family folklore about his mother's shame at having a premature first born, whose impairment, at the time, was considered a fault of parenting. In her mind this shame was compounded later when the family found itself reliant on the WPA, though her husband was in charge of construction for bridges, the Carlisle Hotel among others, and an airport, both independently and under that agency—not exactly the ignominy of being on the dole. But shame is a powerful imprint.

Hawaii

July 1998

In the early stages, my brother's reports on the trajectory of his illness were delivered from 3000 miles and three time zones away. They never came from the weakness of being in a hospital bed, but from an inner strength where he was able to narrate a story about incremental improvements and recovery. The summer we agreed to meet in Hawaii for vacation was the first time I'd witnessed him in decline. The island of Maui has appeared in my mind as dry, windblown, gritty with sand and wretched ever since. It was after one of Mansfield's chemo treatments where they had administered targeted chemicals to cauterize the blood vessels surrounding the cancer in his liver, attempting to starve it of the blood supply that kept it growing. He would return home from these assaults requiring 24-hour monitoring, because the danger of complications from high fevers was so extreme. His friends would rally to cover him in around-the-clock shifts. They would know he was starting to get better when he would kick one of them out for inadvertently snoring or otherwise disturbing his sleep, his old familiar intolerances re-emerging. And slowly his strength would return.

When enough time had passed after one of his treatments, he was able to talk on the phone and said, "I've been near death several times. And then I come to, and I find it's still me, broadcasting from the same wavelength, gazing at the linoleum." His philosophizing and humor were early signals of his return.

He would begin to report that he had been at the pool, sunning himself. Later, he would report triumphantly that he had hiked in Tennessee Valley, made love, begun writing again, and even played tennis. Gradually, he would get his old life back, and with it, bright thoughts about what he could do. He had carefully planned the trip to Hawaii to take place in one of these flowering oases. But this time the shadow of the illness returned sooner than he expected, first showing itself as an inability to eat. By the time I arrived in Maui to join him and Emma, he merely said, "I'm going down again." And he slept most of the day.

The place he had rented for himself and Emma turned out to be not at all like what he'd had on other visits. Rather than a spacious efficiency apartment, this was a cramped sliver of a room looking out on an interior courtyard and pool noisy with kids. He vacillated between irritation at the disturbance and loving their exultant voices shouting out, "Shoot it to the moon, baby!" every time they cannonballed into the water. My room was not much bigger but being a corner unit and looking out on the ocean, it felt more spacious, more like a refuge. I offered to switch rooms, but either he was too proud or the thought of the effort of it exhausted him, and he declined. One night, I made poached salmon and he and Emma came for a sit-down dinner. He held forth, joking at his own expense, and the salmon sat untouched on his plate. Finally, I exploded.

"Can't you say something positive about yourself?" I demanded, as if doing so would be a stake in the ground, a valiant outpost in the battle against encroaching disease, and enough of these could win the war against his cancer. He was stung, and his face broke for a moment into the private vulnerability of a small child.

"I'm trying to make the best of it, to keep it light," he said. "We are on vacation."

"Can't you at least eat your salmon?" I cried back in my rage against his state.

"It tastes like dried cardboard in my mouth," he said quietly.

I saw his misery and knew that I had added to it by assaulting his carefully wrought equanimity. I saw that his even being able to sit at the table was a summoning of will and humor and desire to have another meal with his daughter. I saw that my outburst pushed him closer to the preference for sleep, where the body acquiesced to the silent workings of its own decline.

The next morning, Emma and I sat at the gazebo sipping iced tea, looking out over the ocean while he slept. Still broken-hearted by the pain I had caused him, I said, as if in explanation to myself, "I just can't bear to see him this way." She reached over and put her hand on mine. I felt instantly the knowing she had at 19, of watching this up close over time. She had a heart that could meet mine, and in so doing, she gave me a place for the pain to be.

Joanie

That Mansfield and my younger brother, David, called our mother Joanie when they talked about her implied a distancing from her that I was never quite able to achieve. It was always said with a tinge of irony, suggesting a casual affection and a mocking distance, either of which probably would have been preferred and were being sought even with this small rhetorical device. This was the mother who, in our early childhood, did cartwheels and stood on her head, both of which we pleaded with her to do before we'd allow her to go out in the evening, dressed in a shimmering green or red sheath dress. "Sapphire" was my father's name for her. She read us Winnie the Pooh books and *Charlotte's Web* and *Ferdinand the Bull*, helped us with homework, made clay horses at the Cranbrook Institute and told us stories about her childhood horse, Star-Baby. This was the mother who, as a young teenager, had stolen away from her sister's wedding only to ride back in, moments later, perched atop her horse in her green chiffon dress. "Verve," my aunt, whose wedding this had been, told me after my mother died, "She had verve."

She let us keep frog eggs, so we could watch their amazing hatching process, and, over the years, pet frogs, mice (2, that became 20 overnight), hamsters, guinea pigs, 10 cats, two dogs, two horses, and much later, for my younger sister, Robin, a miniature mule, a Chincoteague pony, and Kalen, the killer white rooster. She took us to *Around the World in 80 Days* and let us watch *The Red Shoes* when we were small and taught us the joys of frequenting the Nugget Theater across the river in Hanover, in the early '60s, when movies were 25 cents for children. As the youngest by seven years of three sisters, she was (at first) the much-adored aunt to their children, our older cousins, who reported her rebelliousness, daring and bad tomboy ways, which had shocked and amazed them.

Our mother loved the Beats, openly admired black men in the 1950s, drew floor plans of dream houses on used envelopes, chain-smoked, toyed endlessly concocting unusual blue and mustard paint colors to try on the walls, frequented junk, thrift and antique stores and, in the process, assembled a collection of antique geared apple peelers among untold other curiosities. She loved the benign hills of Vermont, the rambunctious dirt roads, sudden turns into a pocket of green valley and the broad views across them to Mt. Ascutney or Camel's Hump. She loved a crude wooden oxen bell, the graceful sunburst shape of an old metal disc from an antique industrial fan. A find that particularly thrilled her became our dining room table, the surface of which was a single thick slab of deeply gouged wood that might have been used to slaughter animals on in a former life.

She reveled in her grit, once starting our canvas-top Willis Jeep in the middle of a hill on a patch of sheer ice, spinning the wheels furiously, inching forward until the heat created a grip and the jeep shot forward hurtling around the corner. This was the mother who read constantly, adoring her Iris Murdoch and Doris Lessing, even up to her death underlining and placing bright exclamation points and comments in the margins of Cunningham's *Flesh and Blood*. Legend had it that she turned down an offer for an editing job in New York City at the age of 22 in order to get married in 1947, during the flurry of everybody doing it, following the urge to repopulate the world after World War II.

This was also the mother who would put on *Take Five* to signal, with the sweet abandon of Paul Desmond's sax, that she was going to drink. As a grown-up, it took me years to understand why my whole being flinched at the sound of jazz. In short order, she would be too happy, too festive, fake and wrong to our young and conservative eyes. And I wondered why, even at that young age, I carried a kind of dour prohibition against letting loose, as though I wore a heavy wet cloak that made it impossible to move with any spontaneity or joy, permanently hampered by the sense of being adult way before my time. Even at 11 or 12, I felt the need to parent her reckless ways. The day after she drank, when we were, say, waiting in line stamping our feet in the snow for the annual Ford Sayer ski sale, her eyes would be pink rimmed, puffy and embarrassing, like a flag for all to see, I thought in my infinitely calibrated self-consciousness. The gray miasma that surrounded her marred an eagerly anticipated event. She radiated a dull alarm, the brittle preference to shrink away from being seen in the world. She would be grim and humorless, sunk in the dark residue that remained after the shine of inebriation was long gone.

Within a few years of their divorce, our father visited from Michigan at Christmastime. Our stepfather Dave left to avoid the awkwardness of he and our father feigning politeness for a number of hours in our small living room. There was the novelty of exchanging gifts at night and a kind of forced gaiety that came with celebrating the arrival of our father, who by then felt to me more like a stranger to whom we were vaguely related, since we saw him only a few times a year and my life was lived in the vast immediacy of fourth grade. In the manufactured high spirits, no doubt amplified by our parents' rum laced eggnog, we watched an expansiveness emerge between them that became distinctly playful and flirty. We grew alarmed. We hadn't accepted Dave as our stepfather easily or quickly, but now that we had, we sensed this was a dangerous situation that could in a moment upend our lives again. I watched in a kind of agony as Mansfield stepped up and declared he thought our father should leave. And as our father suddenly became polite and diffident, recognizing that he was on the outside of this family now, banished to the anonymity of a motel room after his long trip by an earnest 11-year-old son. Mansfield was trying to do right, be the man in the family, but it must have stung Dad that this was the same son who faithfully wrote him letters, enthusiastically telling of his exploits and pleading for him to come visit soon.

Once, in 6th grade, I overheard Mansfield and his friend Gordy talking about our mother in the next room. Gordy announced, "She doesn't eat, she drinks!" Everyone laughed at his 13-year-old wittiness, but I felt an inner clutch, at 11, that was my first recognition of shame and the need to hide because of my mother's drinking. A kind of silent interior lock-down moved into place. This was the mother who, after I had conveniently developed a bad cold and demanded to be taken home, returned to my 8th grade graduation party by herself so that she could drink some more. The perennial would-be rebel, she was exultant in her junk-store find of an old license plate that trumpeted, "Repeal the 18th Amendment!" She cleaned it up and, with great fanfare,

nailed it above the lintel on the door in our large kitchen
—a signpost for what was to occur there. It was a decla-
ration of defiance against the very mentality—still alive
and kicking in other domains of 1950s America—that
could conceive such a law.

Brubeck evenings would devolve into loud drunken
nights. A few times, she would storm out, driving off in
a rage into the middle of the night, the house abruptly
silent. There was nothing to be done but huddle in bed
and worry if she would return. One sunny day, we awak-
ened to discover that on the way home from a party the
night before, she and our stepfather, Dave, had flipped
the car over into a ditch, after taking a curve too fast.
Somehow, they had miraculously been able to right it
themselves and drive home. She told the story laughing-
ly, as if it were an emblem of her daring, but we looked
wide-eyed at the whole side of the car covered in
scrapes, dirt and smashed grass that still clung where
they'd been glued on impact.

A gray memory hovers in the limbo of a late winter
afternoon in London, Ontario, where we had moved
following our stepfather to his new job. He was at work.
My mother, incongruously, was in bed. Mansfield was a
thousand miles away at school and David was out with
his friends somewhere. In an oddly languid voice, she
called to me and asked me to come in and rub her back.
I couldn't imagine how to say no. I forced myself to
overcome my 15-year-old allergy to her and a lifetime of
instilled reticence. I suffered from being bred to a long
line of Yankee reserve, calibrating myself to the ongoing
awkwardness of whether I would be hugged by her,
something I recall happening maybe five or six times in
my life. I applied myself to this unfamiliar dark intimacy
with a kind of clinical detachment. I pressed down over
the sheet I'd placed between my hands and her flesh and
leaned into slow circular movements. She asked me to

bring her a large black pill from the shelf in the kitchen, which I did with a glass of water. I sat by her side and continued pressing down on the sacrum area, where she said the pain was. Her voice was too slow and easy. "What a good daughter you are," she said. The statement was uncharacteristic, embarrassing, and something in its global perspective signaled an alarm in me. The stillness in the house was like time suspended. In the long silences between her words, I heard a faint rhythmic sound I could not identify. I became still myself, listening until I recognized the sweet milky breathing of my two-year-old sister, Robin, asleep in the other room. It was like sunshine flooding into me, her perfect pellucid and innocent flesh a lifeline to daylight. I heard another sound and realized our beagle had just sighed and adjusted his position on the floor at the side of Robin's bed, like he would any day. I had regained a sense of perspective.

My mother asked for another pill. I knew it was too soon and said, "Let me go see," putting her off. I went downstairs. I could not reach my stepfather. I counted the pills in the bottle, but realized I had no idea how many she had already taken, but I thought she maybe should not take more. Was she in danger? Had I unwittingly added to it? I debated back and forth, wrestling with myself, and finally called my high school friend's father, who lived down the road and whom I knew was a doctor. In my fear and anxiety, I violated every unspoken rule of privacy, breaching loyalty by talking to another adult and a stranger about my mother, asking for help. She was hospitalized, and we lived three or four months in a palpably lightened air, as though we were adventurers camping, improvising dinners every night with our stepfather. In that interlude of my mother's absence, I was the other adult in the family.

Only three years later, my mother inserted herself

into my personal life, visiting me in Boston, leaving a 5-year-old Robin in my unlocked apartment while she huddled in my older boyfriend's apartment down the block, the two of them conspiring, she later virtuously claimed, to save me from my youthful lapses in judgment. She had left my stepfather and returned to Norwich, Vermont, finding a job once again at Dartmouth—as she had after her first divorce—this time in the height of the student unrest. I got a taste of the extent of her alcoholic delusions when she bragged that she had called Nathan Pusey, the president of Harvard, at 5:30 one of the mornings she stayed with me, ostensibly to discuss the seriousness and urgency of the campus uprisings. Years later, I found out from Robin that when she had left Dave in Canada and returned to Norwich, she had no job or prospects. In the absence of money before she got herself situated, her parents having sold the family farm and moved to elderly retirement housing in New Jersey, she and Robin had lived in a lean-to she had either found or constructed in the woods outside of town. Though I was shocked after the fact on behalf of my sister, I admired my mother's outrageous daring, will and improvisational wherewithal.

I would visit her in my 20s, hoping for a respite in the beloved Vermont hills from the unrelenting concrete, blacktop heat of the inner city, so alien and dispiriting to me. She had migrated north from Norwich to Calais, just outside Montpelier. One time between my own apartment moves, I planned to stay with her for a week. This coincided—or was an excuse for—my mother to go on a bender. I witnessed her drinking around the clock, staying up well into the early morning hours, shouting and singing. She would write and recite impenetrable poetry, pleased with her genius, and carry on conversations with herself, lurching around the house on some important business while Robin and I tried to sleep. She produced her own version of scat, a kind of animated string of cartoon sounds as if she had typed the top row of symbols on a typewriter—!@#$%^&*()_+!—and decided to render each in original sound. Then she would laugh manically at the results she produced. In another context, that might have produced a grudging laugh once, but repeated noisily into the small hours of the night it was enraging, exhausting and ultimately deadening. Her Herculean constitution would mercifully give out under the onslaught, and she would finally peter out into blessed silence. One morning, I got up after a few hours of sleep and nursed a cup of coffee while she was still passed out in the other room. I looked up and noticed Robin's valiant sign, DO NOT DISTURB! hanging from the doorknob of her bedroom. I wanted to laugh and cry at the stalwart spirit who would insist on that flimsy barrier in the face of the force of full-blown alcoholism. As if that could keep at bay the frenzied invasion by her mother each night. Robin's bright instinct for self-preservation asserted itself more strongly later, when she was informally adopted into the family of her closest friends and increasingly spent her time there.

Mansfield visited Vermont only twice in the 35 years after he left high school for San Francisco. The first time was to the Calais house, shortly after our mother's colon cancer surgery, when Dr. Butch, whose name delighted her, told her she had only two years to live. Mansfield would stride off into the wooded hills with his alto sax slung on his back when he could no longer tolerate the thick air and hushed monotony required in her weakened state. When he was in the house, they invariably clashed like two titans—magnets bound to repel each other in their stubborn sameness. During that short visit, my mother's beloved mutt Tammy ran to her death in front of a speeding car on a road she had grown up beside. In the release of my convulsive tears over her limp body, I recall sensing that the dog had run to her death in order to exorcise the negative energy from the house, in the only way her loving spirit knew. It was her final service to my mother.

Mansfield's second visit came many years later. I recall being upstairs at my mother's Cabot, Vermont house late one summer night. This was the house she finally built, after all the drawings on envelopes, after a failed new relationship that had seemed so promising. She had sold her quirky Calais house to move in with this man, only to have it end with the novel explanation that proximity had revealed he suffered from multiple personalities, some of which were apparently intolerable. We suspected that the reverse was more likely the case: that he had discovered her second personality, the demonic one unleashed by alcohol, the one she could keep in check only so long, despite her best intentions.

Earlier that day we all were washing dishes, Mansfield standing out in his low-slung Speedos—his concession to Vermont propriety. My mother's boarder, Mark, was there, happy to have fresh company. In the late evening, the three of us were upstairs; I was in the room above the kitchen, Mansfield and Mark in the room across the hall. We had had a civilized dinner with animated conversation. But my mother had now descended into belligerent drunkenness, getting noisier as the evening progressed. Finally, I got out of bed and went into the room Mansfield and Mark shared. We agreed it was impossible to sleep. We commiserated with Mark who saw a lot more of this, living there. He said it wasn't always this bad. I once again wondered if our presence egged her on, if somehow it was her children she couldn't tolerate. Maybe we reminded her of her mortality or of what she hadn't done in her life because of us. I confessed to them that when I stayed there alone, I often went to sleep fully clothed, sometimes even with my big leather Frye boots on, in case I had to leave suddenly in the middle of the night, though this never happened. We all laughed at the absurd image, belying the very real fear I knew informed me on those occasions. During the day, she mustered her brand of civilized behavior, as though this might be a fresh start. But at night that notion was revealed to be a ploy, as the alcohol let loose a rage of stunning intensity, like some chthonic vortex was opened and she willfully stepped in it to play. It felt as though she was propelled by powerful forces, the way the swimmer in *Jaws* is suddenly and horribly pushed too quickly through the water by the unseen shark below.

I remembered the times I had gone over in my mind how strong she might actually be in such an inebriated state—a pushover or an Amazon? I worried at what might hang in the balance. It was shocking, scary and, in the end, tiring and boring. Later that night, she made love noisily with her boyfriend Harry, as if she was thumbing her nose at us one last time, letting us know she wasn't spent yet. Harry, a gentle, loving and wily soul, was actually allergic to alcohol, becoming ill if he mistakenly ate a small bit of chocolate truffle with a liqueur inside. Nonetheless, he was versed in a lifetime of care-taking his alcoholic brother, so the role came naturally to him.

My mother was the reason there were no formal weddings in our family, though there were two marriages. You never knew what you might get. This was why Mansfield's daughter, Emma, never met her grandmother. Mansfield would not risk that she might be exposed to Joanie's behavior. This was why Mansfield could not tolerate social drinking around him, even his girlfriend Elyse's desire for a single glass of wine with dinner. His own early drug-taking was in the distant past, he had no time for bars, and he considered social drinking a waste of time.

My mother eschewed AA; she could never admit to having a problem with alcohol. Later in her life, while continuing to drink, she improbably worked as a counselor to alcoholics, after putting herself through a Master's degree program at St. Michael's in Vermont. On one occasion, she shyly disclosed to us that she had marshaled a few months without a drink. She sounded embarrassed, almost girlish, clearly prizing what she had accomplished, but stepping gingerly, so as not to break her sobriety as she had so often done, as if it were a rare and precious vase.

She had developed lung cancer almost twenty years after her original bout with colon cancer. She was pronounced free after a regimen of radiation, only to find later that it had metastasized to the brain—a fact discovered after a small, inexplicable rear-ending car accident in which she was at fault. Her obvious lapse in judgment prompted her doctors to order a brain scan. Her death was foreshadowed in an odd incident that occurred on a rare occasion when my younger brother and I were at her house in Cabot, Vermont together. She had looked out her kitchen window, as she always did while washing dishes, and seen the new gleaming white peak of her neighbor's roof. Though she herself had sold her neighbor the land and knew he intended to build, the sight was suddenly unbearable to her. We planted a raft of evergreens to shield her beloved view, but it was as if the assault had already been accomplished, as if she had seen her own death and now carried it as fact within her.

I would often comfort myself by thinking that my mother unfailingly surrounded herself with the most loving animals, as if that were some surviving signpost of her essential goodness. She would be holding forth with a kitten in her lap, perennial cigarette in hand, and watch with delight as the kitten stood up, stretched, stepped onto the table, placed its paw roundly in the middle of her egg yolk, and proceeded on its way. Her animals were never affected by her drinking. Toward the end of her life, she had an aging dog named Babe that she had inherited along the way. Babe lived forever, her strawberry-colored hair growing pale with white and her stiff bones making getting up after one of her long naps a strained and laborious process painful to watch. As my mother lay in a coma at the end of her life, it occurred to me as important to let her know that Babe was fine.

As she was dying, she took to calling me at work. One day, I picked up the phone and there was no one on the line, but the line was live. I instantly understood that she had found the wherewithal to punch in the numbers, but no longer had the wherewithal to speak. I stayed on the phone saying a few comforting phrases to her, told her I would be up to visit her soon, then hung up.

David and I convened in Montpelier, near where she had formerly lived and where our sister Robin had gone to high school at U32. We called our mother from a pay phone to let her know we were on the last leg of the trip and would soon be there. She flat-out barred us from her house. She was fierce. "Don't you dare come up here!" she commanded, like a she-wolf protecting her den. We proceeded anyway, winding our way east on Route 2. We stopped at Rainbow Sweets in Marshfield, her favorite bakery, with heavenly empanadas, pastries and cakes. We chatted with the gregarious owner, who sometimes got his eggs from Harry, my mother's boyfriend. But I found myself being careful about mentioning her, sensitive in my hyper-emotional state to any comments he would feel no compunction against saying, that would relegate her to town drunk status. I so wanted someone to remember her bright side. We got two of the most opulent cake slices we could find and continued on to her house.

In the hubbub of our arrival, she forgot her prohibition. She fell on the cake, eating it greedily as though she'd just discovered a nutrient she'd been without her whole life. I was surprised, recalling that she had never had a sweet tooth, had disdained sweets except for the rare periods when she was sober. Of course, by then she was stone sober. She seemed vulnerable, like she was a child, uncertain of herself around us, almost polite. We were solicitous of her. At one point David attempted to draw her out about whether her affairs were in order, whether she had made the necessary provisions for her estate. She acted defensive and hurt, as though at a loss to answer such rudely overt questions. I could see David was being loving in his way: diligent, matter-of-fact, concerned that she not be left vulnerable in her compromised state. She made a mute appeal to me and I squirmed a moment before deflecting the question with some palliating comment suggesting we could get to that later, knowing we would not. I acquiesced to her, thinking we should let her go the way she wanted. As it turned out, we discovered soon enough that she was perfectly explicit in her will, leaving her assets evenly divided between her four children with nothing going to Harry, the man she loved, who was in the room with us at the time of that truncated conversation.

The night she died I received a call from the hospital alerting me that they thought the end was near. It had been one of those remarkably warm January days, a true Indian summer where the 45 degrees feels more like Honolulu than New England. I jumped in my car and headed north toward Vermont. Near Manchester, New Hampshire, I noticed the windshield would not clear, pulled off the road to use my scraper, and realized I was standing on a covering of ice that had suddenly formed like the glaze on a cake. I sidled back into the car and crept to the first exit, mercifully close, and into a Ramada Inn just off the ramp. It was past midnight by the time I checked-in. When I finally made it into my room, exhausted, I faced head-on two historical etchings: one of Morgan stallions, the other Morgan mares and fillies. It was like looking at a message straight from the heart of my mother. She revered Morgan horses; her horse Star-Baby was a Morgan, and she had taught me to love and admire them almost worshipfully from an early age. Seeing the mares and fillies, something broke in me and there was a washing away, a lifting, as if all was forgiven, both ways. I talked with the loving and thoughtful nurses periodically until 2:00 a.m., when they told me my mother had died.

Bob

April 2, 2001

Fran's husband Bob came to spend time with Mansfield last night. Mansfield slept and Bob sat like a sentinel, perfectly contained and imperturbable, with his back to the window. He was absolutely erect, a posture I mistakenly took for a familiar sort of Yankee rectitude or reserve. I was a bit intimidated, unsure how to approach him until he opened his mouth and came out with one of his dry, outrageously hilarious and irreverent observations. Bob was the master of understatement, his deadpan delivery the perfect foil to whatever was to come.

Twenty-two years earlier, Bob found himself in one of Fran's art classes and, as he told it, promptly decided to marry her. Thirteen years her junior, he improbably succeeded—for which, he would periodically announce, he was eternally blessed. After Mansfield's death, he, Fran, Paul, and Tereza treated me to dinner, honoring their bet with Mansfield that Bush would win the White House. The debt had to be paid by proxy posthumously because Mansfield had no longer been able to eat a meal nor sit up long enough when the debt came due. Bob made a general announcement to the table about the beauty of his wife, the staggering good fortune he enjoyed because of his ongoing association with her, and

his everlasting gratitude for both. All of this was delivered in his easy, steady, even-keeled way, as though it
grew up from the very earth of his body. Then Paul
began extolling Tereza's fine qualities, though he admitted at first she'd rebuffed his overtures for a dance.
Tereza could be formidable and was the night he met her
at the Haight Street club, demonstrating a signature
Latina sovereignty. Paul had simply said, "Did you come
here to dance or what? It's only a dance, I'm not going
to marry you!" She was so taken aback that she got up
and danced with him. And that was that. I was moved by
these men's open celebration of their women.

Jonathan

April 3, 2001

Jonathan comes by around noon. Luckily Mansfield's
energy is up and he is lucid. I can tell that he has looked
forward to this visit, though I sense a tension. Perhaps
it was only the novelty of expectation. I know there are
times when Jonathan showed up a few hours later than
they agreed, and Mansfield was deeply disappointed,
frustrated that he had to go back to sleep and then was
unable to rally himself when Jonathan did arrive. Yet I
knew there was a longer history too. When Mansfield
was well, he wouldn't bother to drive to Emeryville,
where Jonathan had bought a place, insisting instead on
being visited in Mill Valley. Maybe this was residual
habit from the group houses where people had naturally
congregated in his domain. It was a considerable cross-
town hike for Jonathan and undoubtedly caused a low-
lying sense of contention between them.

I've heard endless stories about Jonathan and met

him twice before over the years. Seeing him again only reanimates the folklore my brother has created around him. One of his other names is The Tusker, which pretty faithfully captures the gestalt of his presence. Jonathan is bald, tall, broad-chested, searingly smart, quirkily funny and with a powerful physical presence. My brother complains that, when they sit in a café, it is not uncommon for women to interrupt them and actually turn their backs on Mansfield completely in order to blatantly proposition Jonathan. When Mansfield's illness gave him his first shot at baldness and women accosted him, too, he kicked himself for not figuring out the appeal of baldness years earlier.

I recognize a kind of torque between them, like bringing together two generators, and see why my brother treasures their friendship. Their conversation is fast, competitive, filled with references to their shared knowledge and subject matter cultivated over the years. Despite my best intentions, I revert to the posture of an awkward schoolgirl. I can't comment on the subtleties of the Heart Sutra or Kabir, so I busy myself making tea and listen instead.

Later, when trying to explain to Fran my sense of stumbling around Jonathan, she said that, though she's been a close friend of his for years, she understood completely. She described a time when Jonathan demonstrated his penchant for the orthogonal comment. He called her and, when she answered the phone, proclaimed, "Well, and there you are!" as though that was sufficient to beginning, middle and end of conversation and nothing more need be said. Then he hung up.

Susan

April 5, 2001

Susan, Emma's mother, comes to visit in the late morning. Mansfield is up and expecting her. He sits cross-legged at the foot of his mattress, facing the door with an equanimity honed over years. She sails in, big breasted, eyes shining, an entourage unto herself. She is dressed for business in her current man-style suit and bow-tie. "Oh, Popsie.......look at you! I love you so! Oohhh.....Why did you have to go and get sick on us?" she says. I see Mansfield's resolve falter, as though finally defeated by the now superior force of an old combatant. He closes his eyes and tears stream down his face as he gives in and submits to her attentions.

Mirror

April 6, 2001

I look up from my tea and can just see at an angle into the bathroom. Mansfield stands before the mirror and observes himself. He turns sideways and brings his arm up to flex his muscles. Where once his flesh was rounded and opulent, now it is wan, thin and flat, as if there no longer is any muscle there at all. I turn away quickly, not wanting to intrude on his privacy, not able to be still in the anguish of the moment. He comes out of the bathroom and prepares for sleep, saying nothing.

The hospice psychologist

April 10, 2001

The hospice psychologist comes infrequently so each visit is an occasion. Her role is somewhat mysterious and I somehow feel as if we are being tested. I am never sure if Mansfield or I pass the test, though I am always left with a residual sense that we are lacking in some essential way. And I never quite know why I am in her conversations with Mansfield. Our talk feels as though it should be leading somewhere, but that it rarely seems to get there, or has any real substance. Mansfield confesses privately, however, to having the hots for her. Since he's been bemoaning his illness-induced loss of libido, I think this is to be celebrated, even if my allegiance is to Elyse. The psychologist is tall and thin with long, wavy black hair. She dresses tastefully, in a kind of Marin County artistic chic. Mansfield, as is his way, embraces her in greeting. Thin as he is, he can still enfold her within his arms. He steps back suddenly and says, "Oh! It's like hugging myself!" She blushes and they both laugh at the parity between the illness-induced thinness of his body and the fashionable thinness of hers.

The three of us sit in a protracted silence at the end of our rambling, desultory conversation. Then Mansfield, almost as if voicing a private soliloquy to himself says, "I feel as if I'm getting better, but it's taking...... so.......long!" His voice is forlorn, as if he can't quite make out why that is, and despairs of ever doing so. I see her mouth drop open in disbelief that, after all his philosophical talk about acceptance of death, this is what he comes home to in his heart. It is as though the mind cannot give up the possibility of hope even as it struggles with the ever-present tedium of sure decline. The stunned silence lasts a minute and is gone, his comment unanswered.

Reverie

April 12, 2001

This morning Mansfield looks up out of his own private reverie. He says, "Elyse is the finest woman I've ever known. She's beautiful, smart, loving, with it, sophisticated. She's a savvy business woman, sexy... she's....she's everything!" He pauses, considering. "I don't know why I didn't live with her." In this moment of lucidity, he contemplates his confounding self with a kind of wonder. "You could tell her that," I offer.

Zen Guy

April 13, 2001

Zen Guy says he is coming, and we are in a state of delighted anticipation. He has lived in Thailand for years and was Mansfield's connection when he went there, his conduit to the comings and goings of other friends who regularly passed through. I received photos of Mansfield spread-eagled in front of a golden Buddhist temple, crouching with a startling intensity in his green eyes amidst row upon row of gilded Buddhas, and posturing in a forest of massive lingams swathed in colorful banners, straining for the sky, proclaiming the fertility they offered. I'd heard his stories of how he put that energy to use sojourning in Phuket, and later read more explicit details of these accounts in one of his manuscripts. Zen Guy has only recently returned to San Diego, and he and Mansfield haven't seen each other in years. I first get an email from him politely asking when would be a good time to drop in. After all these years of hearing stories about him, his full name printed at the top of the page: Paul White, feels banker-ish.

When he arrives, a quiet presence seems to enter the room before him like a change in air before the weather turns for the better. Emma is here for a quick visit, and they plan to talk about Japan, South Korea, and Thailand, helping her decide where she should teach English her first year out of college. Eventually I leave them to their private conversation and drive up to the Depot Cafe in the center of Mill Valley to look at people and see a different set of walls. When I return, more than two hours later, I am astonished to see they are all still here and Mansfield wide awake and sitting up. There is a sense of fullness and contentment, as though they have touched on everything important and yet there is still more.

I recall a story Jonathan told, describing a time years before when, in their early twenties, they all worked on a painting crew where an enormous black man was foreman. They were up on scaffolding, working on a house where a beautiful woman lived, a creature who commanded their attention and was the subject of their private deliberations. As they joked around, debating who was going to score with her and how, their pal Zen Guy showed up down below, strolling with her on his arm. The foreman turned to them and declared authoritatively, "He Mister Delicious Man," as if nothing more need be said. The name stuck.

Wide awake at 2:00 a.m.

April 14, 2001

Sometimes Mansfield's internal clock is turned around and he just needs to be up in the middle of the night. His accumulated sleep catches up with him and he is fully awake, looking for something to do. One morning, we sit in a small pool of yellowy light in his office, him in the oak swivel chair at his desk, me in a chair on casters nearby. At 2:00 a.m., it is profoundly dark and still. With everyone around us in the complex asleep, there is a novelty to being up, as though outside the bounds of reality. We are in a different room—not the front room where he sleeps, not my office where I sleep, and it is almost as though he is not sick. We are not bound by daytime realities. We could have been just meeting anywhere to talk, except for the night pressing thickly in on us. I discover that, though he does not drink, he keeps a bottle of brandy high up on a shelf in his office closet—to help him sleep, he says. We pour a tiny amount and share it. The talk is slow, meandering. We talk about Julie, his high school girlfriend from more than 30 years before, whose image filled his early paintings. Now, he says, she is living in Oregon, doing something with radio. I remind him of our first truly independent trip, when he was allowed to drive our grandfather's old maroon Oldsmobile pick-up truck, provided I would go as chaperone, to visit Julie at her parent's house on the Housatonic River in western Connecticut. It was the summer of 1966, when he was working road construction for Perini on Route 91. All the way to Julie's house, we listened to "Bald-Headed

Lena," "Under My Thumb" and "Satisfaction" on the radio, as though they were anthems of this new country we were entering. I recalled so keenly the fresh sense of summer, infinitely expanding possibility, and then, at Julie's house, the sweet domesticity of waking early in a strange place with two seemingly happy parents and the sound of the river constantly, busily moving by.

Our talk turns to a man named Hazen, who had lived for a brief time with his wife and young son in a small cabin up the hill from our grandfather's barn. Mansfield thought that Hazen had been unable to recover from having been in World War II, and our grandfather helped him out with a place to live and odd jobs for a time. Mansfield, Hazen and Daddy Harry would periodically go with the chain saw to clear brush in the woods. All I remembered was how thin and wiry and nice he was, his definitive stride coming around the corner of the barn, and how suddenly empty it was when he was gone.

Two

April 15, 2001

Mansfield looks up and says, "It's so crowded in here!"

"Oh, how is that?" I ask.

"Well, there's two of everyone. Two of you, two of me, two of Dad, two of Daddy Harry, two of Damma."

"Oh....what's the second me like?" I ask, ever self-absorbed.

"It's just the other you," he says as though it is an obvious and known phenomenon, needing no further clarification. I muse on the oddly crowded party at-

mosphere this evokes, not mentioning that of the five—
or ten—of us, only he and I are alive.

Years ago, camping on Vancouver Island when I was
20, I sat on the open tailgate of the jeep, gazing at the
earth at my feet in idle contemplation. In a vertiginous
moment, my perception flipped, and I saw a complex
matrix of angulated relationships between every in-
finitesimal stone, pebble, grain of sand, twig and fallen
leaf. A web of pulsating existence was revealed, infinitely
beautiful and alive. I found I could move my eyes and go
back and forth between these two realities, before I
looked up and carried on with the necessity of making
dinner. When Mansfield saw all those people, I thought
maybe he was seeing into a matrix self, the particular
template construction that holds together the idea of
this particular flesh, this existence, at any given point in
time.

Jeff

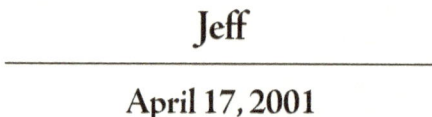

April 17, 2001

This morning, after we finish breakfast, the construction site across the way is alive with men and vehicles
coming and going. A truck pulls up below our window
in order to back into the site to drop off its load. The
sun slants down against the windshield slightly obscur-
ing the driver in a dapple of reflected sun and shadow.
"It's Jeff!" Mansfield exclaims. He becomes agitated
with excitement. "It's my buddy, Jeff," he says. He paces
to the window, then kneels down to where the small
casement opened out to the street below. "Jeff!!......
Jeff!" he calls. His toothpick body is folded in a crouch
and his bald head from behind shows the eagerness of a

child. I cannot bear to see where his mind has gone, nor to bring him back. "It might not be him," I say tentatively. He gazes at the truck, watching it angle back into the narrow driveway. He turns away in disappointment, resigning himself to preparing for his day of sleep.

I call Jeff in LA to tell him how eager Mansfield was when he thought he saw him. Luckily, I find him at work. His wife's jealousy is legendary. He once told her he was going to a conference in Seattle in order to spend a few days with Mansfield.

"I'm so glad you told me that," he says. "I've got to get up there and spend some time with him."

"Come soon," I say.

Peculiar behavior: 2:00 a.m.

April 18, 2001

I hear something that awakens me at 2:00 a.m. and stumble out of bed. I find Mansfield in the bathroom, his large shoulders and back straining to pull the medicine cabinet out of the wall. "What do you want!?" I cry. "Cereal," he says.

"Oh ... I'll make it for you in the kitchen."

"OK," he agrees, and follows me around the corner.

I need to be watching him more closely, once again. I discover uncooked oatmeal in with the Wheat Chex and Grapenuts he is making himself. I wonder how that might gum up the works, but four hours later he merely says, "I'm really thirsty." I discover the milk carton open on both ends like a square cylinder in the shelf with the cereal, and the cardboard oatmeal container wet with water and placed in the rack to dry. He devises various ploys for opening soda cans that involve using spoons for levers. When that doesn't work, he stabs at the top with a knife and then drinks out of a mean-looking ripped metal hole.

Late afternoon outing

April 19, 2001

Late in the day, Mansfield can get a burst of energy, as though the sheer tedium of sleeping is more than his body and mind can bear. Today, he begins pulling on his pants, shoes and jacket. At first I think he is just amusing himself, finding something different to do. Then he surprises me by declaring, "I'm going for a walk." I scramble to collect my jacket and keys and follow him out the door. Starting down the stairs, he begins to stumble and I become worried he will fall. I position myself ahead of him, where I think I can catch him, or at least break his fall. He sees what I am doing and forbids me to be in front of him. He orders me to go down and wait at the bottom of the steps. Once down, he lurches over the pavement toward the new construction, in what looks like an impulse of pure will power. He is so thin and uncertain on his legs that he really does look like what he calls himself: an egg on stilts. There is an extreme vulnerability that makes him beautiful, as though he is translucent. I curse the speed bumps on the pavement that might be hazardous to his progress but dare not give him my shoulder to lean on. Two deer, the ones we saw earlier out the window, wander grazing near the new houses—close and with an assuredness that they have more right to be there than we. A strong smell of chemical—like a lacquer or nail polish—hits us from the construction site. Probably overreacting, I worry about the effect of these chemicals on his already damaged liver. When we come back around, he says, "I've got to get out of here. Let's take a drive."

I run upstairs, grab the emergency meds bag, and meet him back at the car. We head out Tennessee Valley Road, sweeping around the languid curves, the long lines of sunlight glancing through the thicket of trees. We park in the almost empty lot, facing the trail to the ocean, the horse farm to our left. "Let's just sit," he says. He cracks the window and pulls a flattened pack of Camels from his shirt pocket. "Cigarettes!?" I say. "Yep," he says with authority. I haven't smoked in years, and he "doesn't" smoke. He pulls out a book of matches and lights up. We pass the cigarette back and forth, sharing it like old conspirators. It is a delicious, forbidden taste. We roll the windows down, lean back in our seats and gaze out on the broad hills rising up in a bulwark around us, protecting us from the ocean. Thin eucalyptus groves follow the meandering path before us, as though a stream once flowed there allowing them to take root. We see occasional deer, small, barely perceptible in the distance against the scrub hill until a faint suggestion of movement catches the eye.

"This is like sneaking out for a butt behind the barn," I say, "I feel like I'm getting stoned." We recall other perfect smoking moments: at The Farm, in his bedroom above our grandfather's room, at the end of a long hot day's work when he worked road construction, in high school, out behind a building where we'd congregate to meet our friends.

"Remember when everybody was smoking Gauloises? Who knows where we even got them? They were so strong it was like getting stoned. Or those American Indian's or those herb-flavored things that were so gross?" There is an old thrill of complicity in that sense of stopped time, sitting side by side, busily doing nothing.

He turns toward me. "If I die tomorrow......" he begins.

I am about to say, "I hope you don't," then catch myself and say, "I hope you do exactly what you want." He pauses, looks away, and then says, "Thank you." We sit in silence watching the light recede from the sky. It gets that high, dark jewel-like quality.

"Let's go," he says. I start up the car and we roll back down the hill, lazy on the curves, the only car on the road in the gathering dusk.

He turns to me and says, "Don't tell Emma."

"What?" I ask, thinking I missed something.

"About the cigarette," he says.

"Oh ... OK," I say, struck by the reminder of his strictness with himself in the example he sets as a father, even now, in this context. I want to protest that she would understand, but respect the firmness of his resolve and, at the same time, want to laugh at the absurdity of the situation. We park and head up the stairs.

"I've got to get out of this trough," he says, as though reminding himself to pay a persistent creditor.

It is only later that I awaken to what I missed. I see again how he turned toward me, open and ready, and I cut him off mid-sentence, mid-gesture, in the sleepwalking state of my automatic response. It was as definitive as if I'd snipped a flower off at the bud. I did not find the stillness, the spaciousness inside me to hear him. What expression did I deny him in doing that? I had no idea what it was that was important to him if he died tomorrow. I would never know, even if I could walk into the other room, shake him awake and plead for him to remember what it was he wanted to say. It was the first time that we had spoken in the present of his sense of his own dying that was not a joke or a philosophical musing about it, and I was asleep to it. No, I was actively deflecting it. I saw how my own fear held me back.

Urgency at 2:00 a.m.

April 21, 2001

I awaken to a commotion in the next room. I jump off my palette and find Mansfield trying to get into the closet without knowing how to open it. He is leaning against the wall, clawing at the sliding doors in a desperate, mad-scrabble way. His urgency is extreme. I am bewildered, until I suddenly realize he needs to go to the bathroom and has gotten lost en route. I grab the device Margaret had given us that we had laughed at, considering it useless. It is a plastic cylinder with a wide and angled neck. I place it under him and say, "You can go now." He puts his arm on the wall, leans his head against his arm and just lets go, peeing for long minutes while I hold the vessel to him. His relief is palpable—not just that he can pee, but that he has preserved civility— he has not peed on the rug, the wall, himself, has not descended into the indignity of complete loss of bodily control.

Fran and the white wolf

April 23, 2001

I drive home from errands that I was doing during one of Fran's visits, to find the house empty. I am surprised, as it is normally a sleep time for Mansfield. I decide to look for them and discover them sitting side-by-side up the scrubby hill that leads to the bluff overlooking the complex—a place I've never been. I scrabble up to sit beside them and am amazed that Mansfield negotiated the steep crumbly ascent. We sit in the dried grasses, savoring the sun on our faces, surveying the valley below and the abrupt hill beyond, which, with the one we are sitting on, serve as topographical bookends for the meandering Tennessee Valley.

The conversation is quiet, like a random murmur, until Mansfield suddenly says, "Look! Over there!" He points to the high slatted fence surrounding a yard below. "I think it's a wolf. It's a white wolf!" he says. Through a break in the fence, I can see a white sheet billowing softly in the occasional breeze. The three of us watch in silence. "It's probably just a trick of the eye," I offer tentatively. "No! I think it's trying to get out," he says, becoming agitated. "See, it's moving around!" We all watch again, Mansfield's concern rising. Finally, Fran says, "Well, I think we should go down there and investigate."

We muster ourselves and form a phalanx. Mansfield, still with a terrified look on his face, walks between us. We slowly and carefully traverse the uneven terrain, approaching the yard below. Mansfield's fear is not allayed. He has seen a cunning wild beast, a fierce predator bent on getting out, and this reality is stamped on him, his whole being instinctively mobilized in alarm against the threat.

Whether the images recompose themselves to reveal the pedestrian sheet, or whether moving across the hill so fatigues him, the question of the white wolf dissipates. We veer off and head back to the darkened room so he can sleep. I have a sense of disappointment that we've seen laundry rather than a wild beast, and I prefer to shrink from the recognition that Mansfield's brain is affected, might even be riddled with cancer. Later, Fran tells me that when she arrived, he said to her, "I have to get out of here. I'm in this room, but it's not this room." "You mean you have to will yourself out of here?" she asked. "That would imply consciousness," he replied.

John

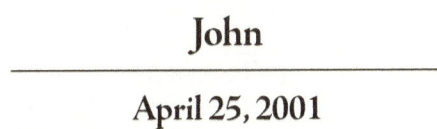

April 25, 2001

John comes, all the way from Ashland, Oregon. I have heard his name forever. Mansfield was looking forward to his visit, but it turns out he is having a particularly low day. He sleeps all day and cannot rouse himself even though he knows John is here. For some reason, I just can't bear to see his decline keeping him from the beloved friend he now sees so rarely. I sit in my office, pinioned against the wall in front of my computer, as John puts his head in the door. I explain to him how eager Mansfield was to see him. Mansfield loves John like a younger brother, and is ever grateful that John convinced him, one day after tennis in Sausalito, that he could work for himself, make more money and have more independence running his own painting crews.

Mansfield did just that: moved from the inner city to Mill Valley, and built a thriving business that gave him independence and the flexibility to continue his art. He kicked himself for not doing so years earlier. He reveled in daily access to the ocean, walks in the Marin hills. I proceed to tell John the stories Mansfield has told me about him, wanting to convey Mansfield's love, his enthusiasm at the prospect of seeing him—trying to make up for Mansfield's absence, until I disintegrate in tears. It feels absurd that John comforts me, when I was trying to take care of him, and I cry more. With extraordinary grace and presence, John tells me his love for Mansfield is so solid that nothing is lost. Then he tells me about his new life in Ashland, where he moved with his wife and kids, and invites me to visit them there whenever I can.

I can do this too

April 26, 2001

In the middle of the night, I waken suddenly to see that the light is on. I wrench myself out of bed and into the other room. It is 4:00 a.m. and I noticed the 2:00 a.m. anti-emetic syringe dose untouched in its glass. A pool of glistening vomit is soaking into the rug beside Mansfield's mattress. "Oh God," I say to him. "Take this now." I put the syringe to his mouth and he sucks the pink goop out of it hungrily. "I'll clean that up in the morning," I say wearily. Mansfield sits up and points to the mess urgently. His hand, like a gun, makes a perfect "You Are Here" sign. He cannot make the words anymore, but he leans his head down close to his pointing finger and his intention is clear. He wants it cleaned up right away. I turn into the kitchen and get a bowl of water and a sponge. I scrub at the slimy mess, barely containing my own impulse to heave. I am so angry at being dominated into this demeaning task at 4:00 a.m. that I have tears in my eyes. Yet I respect my brother's insistence on civility and self-respecting behavior, the clear line drawn against his descent into loss of control and degradation of life. I think, "I can do this, too."

Sundowners

April 27, 2001

Mansfield is beginning to get more restless agitation at night. It frightens me. I awaken last night to an unfamiliar sound. It is around 4:00 a.m., and when I get to the front room, I find him on his hands and knees, with the front door open, trying to crawl out onto the balcony. He is determined, willful, as if he just wants to go but can't quite make it all the way out. I feel he might be stronger than I am and that I might not be able to pull him back. But when I say, "Let's get back into bed," he allows himself to be guided back inside. I feel lucky. He could just as easily ignore me, and I wouldn't be able to do anything. Margaret tells me later, when I relay the experience to her, that it is not unusual. It is a syndrome called "sundowners" that can occur as people come closer to their death. It is a sort of body knowing that something in the turn just before dusk or dawn offers a way through to another dimension, an easier way to leave. Maybe it's the will practicing the intention to leave. The fear of it, the need for hyper-vigilance exhausts me. I begin to think I need help at night.

A hospice worker
and her daughter

April 30, 2001

Maggie, a Marin Hospice worker comes to spell me, and she wants something to read to fill the time as Mansfield sleeps. She pulls the *Eden Warriors* manuscript from the shelf and, just as Mansfield is falling asleep, asks him if she can read it. When I return, hours later, she can barely tear herself away from it. "I almost feel as if I'm tripping," she says, "...I mean, read this." She hands me the manuscript pointing to a paragraph:

In his measured British precision, Robin Trower's lead guitar soared through the stratosphere in cosmic lament, raking the synapses of forty thousand acidheads, delivering them to the gates of eternity. Jerry Abram's headlights worked the light-show, projecting pulsating amoebas, footage from open-heart surgery, unearthed skeletal remains, and electron microscope takes on the double helix of DNA. Our senses were overloaded to ecstatic saturation, and our minds bloomed with archetypes. We had been transformed into tribal shamans, risking total madness to taste the nectar of altered states. The pungent aroma of clouds of marijuana wafted through the crowd of tie-dyed shirts and incredibly long, wild hair. New world gypsies danced in frenzied intoxication with sexually explosive nymphets wearing almost nothing. Black lights cast an eerie lunar glow through a maze of faces painted with day-glo paint, and strobe lights flashed with a haunting regularity that tended to invoke epileptic seizures...... Robin Trower's liquid metal lead guitar cascaded through the sustained tears of the lysergic blues, a slow-hand echo of the brilliance of Jimi Hendrix.

"I was here then," she says. "It was just like that. I feel as if I'm back there again ..... I mean there's stuff about Grace Slick, McLaughlin, Quicksilver Messenger, Santana, Shankar ... everything. I feel as if I'm reliving it." She continues talking, reluctant to break the spell.

After she leaves, later in the evening, she calls, saying that her 20-year-old daughter wants to interview Mansfield about his early San Francisco days, for an article she wants to write. I know Mansfield will be tickled by such avid interest from a stranger Emma's age. I also know he can no longer sit up nor stay awake long enough for it to happen. I talk to the daughter and feel her disappointment, her mother's and my own. We all want more—more stories, more questions answered, more explanations, more life. I feel the dissonance of wanting to hear more about his life, even as he is wholly absorbed in his dying, the door already closing, as if life is saying, no, this is what we are doing now, walking down this dark inexorable ever-narrowing path.

Elyse's vacation

May 1, 2001

Elyse is torn. She has scheduled a vacation—it's been on her calendar for months. I tell her I think he is going to die soon and that, of course, only makes her feel worse. Margaret is encouraging her to go. She says it could be tomorrow or a month from now, and that she should go because she desperately needs the rest.

Dr. Pond comes again

May 5, 2001

Mansfield has been so restive again, as if looking for a way out of life. Margaret tells me Dr. Pond is coming this morning, and I tell Mansfield. He can't speak and does not register any reaction to what I say, but I know he understands. It is as though, deep within him, something focuses, coalesces around the impending encounter. It is a bright sunny morning. Dr. Pond arrives early. Mansfield has roused himself, waiting. To relieve the pressure he feels in his abdomen, he kneels on the floor, his head resting on his hands, butt in the air. Dr. Pond says, "Mansfield, it's good to see you." Mansfield doesn't say anything, but he shifts his weight slightly so that he can slide one arm beneath his belly and shake Dr. Pond's hand. He is recognizing his old ally. Dr. Pond is down on the floor beside him. "It won't be long now," he says gently. With that, Mansfield leans to the side and lets himself fall into Dr. Pond's arms. He is cradled, like an enormous child, inside the arc of Dr. Pond's body. Dr. Pond strokes the length of his arm, again and again. I stand to the side, tears streaming down my face.

Fragility

May 6, 2001

I have such a strong sense of the fragility of Mansfield's life and the minute-to-minute imminence of his death. I feel like a fretful mother, wanting to hover and attend to his smallest need—though I know he can't stand that. I feel so physically tethered to this apartment, to this room, the utter innerness of this time. Fran and Bob invited me for dinner last night. I know I should have gone and yet felt an overwhelming reluctance. Part of it was my fear of driving to somewhere new—across the Golden Gate and the Bay Bridge for the first time alone at night and admonished myself for indulging an old phobia. Yet a part of me insists on sitting vigil. I turned down my friend Joanne's invitation to her birthday dinner last week, unable to imagine myself turning my attention to pleasantries and current events among strangers.

Paul, Margaret, Mansfield
and Me

May 7, 2001

Paul comes in the morning. Margaret is already here. She helps me prop Mansfield up on a mountain of pillows. It makes his breathing easier; the slight gravity helps drain away the liquid that sounds in his lungs. Mansfield is heavy in his medicated stupor and, though he looks wraithlike, his bones weigh him down. The mound of pillows is unstable in the middle of his bed; he keeps sinking down into it, and then his breathing suffers again. "I wish we had a hospital bed," I say. "You know we tried," says Margaret, reminding me of his adamant refusal to permit any addition to his possessions.

Paul lifts Mansfield up and places him against the pillows whenever he slides down. Margaret and I sit at the low table in front of the window, again going over the precise schedule of medications. She is encouraging me, telling me I can administer anal suppositories, there is nothing to it. While we go over the new schedule, Paul kneels by Mansfield's side and talks to him with the easy familiarity of someone who's been a close brother for more than 30 years. He talks to him as though Mansfield and he are the only ones in the room, and Mansfield is present and understands every word. Paul encourages him, saying, "Mansfield! Go for the light!" as if he were a loving chorus, cheering him on. He tells Mansfield he loves him. I am humbled by what he knows to do, his gentle, strong presence, the simple, direct assertion of his love, his open-heartedness.

꙰ ꙰ ꙰

After they both leave, the sound of Mansfield's breathing remains, deep and labored. I keep returning to his side, fretting. At one point in mid-afternoon, I run my hand across his arm, as if to say, "It's OK." But I feel repelled, as if his cells are ordering me to leave him alone, that it requires every ounce of his being to concentrate on doing the work at hand. I am not only a distraction, but he knows in my fear I might want to hold him here. Later I say, "It's OK to go now if you want." My words are tentative: I have no idea what I am talking about or what to do or say. In desperation, I call the hospice nurse's assistant to see if she can come early but am told by her daughter that she is taking a nap in preparation for her night shift.

Mansfield has sunk lower into the pillows, and it looks like excruciatingly hard work for him to breathe. I think of the neighbor up the hill, who might help me prop him up higher again, but there is no answer when I call. I wonder how it can be so hard. It seems his body is a powerful machine that will not be turned off, despite the considerable force of his will. His breathing slows. The effort wracks him. He is still for an impossibly long time. Then a great gasp of an in-breath shudders through his body, almost an after-thought, almost lost. His chest heaves and he growls, his lips curling back. My own breathing distorts to match his. I stand up and pace back and forth in front of him in my agitation. I feel an overwhelming urge to ululate. It wants to bust out of me. It is as though my body knows it would relieve the overwhelming pressure I feel, and also provide a corridor of sound for him that might be a pathway out. I make some tentative sounds, then looking at the intense inward focus on his face think, if he could speak he might want to say, "Will you just shut up!" I want to fling open the door and shout, "Someone please come help me here now!" Instead, I kneel in front of him again, studying him minutely. I listen to each lengthening pause between breaths. Another pause comes and I then watch a distinct line simply pass across his lips, like the last ray of sun moving across a field before night sets in. There is nothing more.

The telephone next to the bed rings. I answer it automatically, without taking my eyes off him. I am grateful to hear my sister Robin's voice. "He just died, not a minute ago," I say. Instantly I feel a pang of worry that I might have made a mistake. I touch his arm, as if that could tell me something. Robin's voice comforts me. We muse on the depth of her connection with him, even though he was already away at high school when she was born. How did she know, in the long stretch of months, to call just at the moment of his death? When we hang up, I continue studying him, still looking for some hint of life, having to be sure. I allow 10 minutes to pass, then lift the phone and call Fran. We divvy up telephone calls and put the word out.

Within a few hours, people begin to congregate. First Fran and Bob, then Lightnin', Susan, Mansfield's stalwart neighbor Jean. Calls keep coming in. More calls are made. We are sprawled around the room, moving in and out of the kitchen. People bring wine and beer, the first time I've ever seen it in Mansfield's domain. That is quickly gone, and someone runs out to get more. Everyone is telling stories. Bob holds forth with his particular brand of hilarious irreverence that keeps everyone giddy with laughter. Someone notices that as we have been talking, Mansfield has changed. The planes of his face have smoothed, become luminous, the pain and effort that had contorted them gone. He looks ethereal, lying back on his bank of pillows, as though his whole being has gathered and is emitting a soft light.

A few hours later, a nurse comes. She is required to pronounce him officially dead. She gives precise instructions on what is to be done with his remaining drugs and is gone. Near midnight, a knock at the door interrupts our stories. A man walks in—dark black, perfectly shaped and impeccably dressed in a black suit. He shows exacting and deferential courtesy, and quietly commands the room.

"I am sorry to disturb you so late," he says. "I am here to attend to the deceased." He introduces himself as from Pacific Interment. I remember Mansfield telling me with delight that they found this alternative way to manage a cut-rate death without the heavy overlay of a funeral home, and how Jonathan put everything in place more than a year ago. And now here it is, happening perfectly. A tall lithe pale-skinned black woman steps into the room behind the man. He introduces her and states, "She will assist me." The woman, dressed as he is in black, gives a brief almost imperceptible bow, acknowledging the room of us, and stands beside him, poised respectfully. He explains what they need to do in detail, as though the saying of it will lessen the shock that they are proposing taking Mansfield's body away from us. We are so taken with the theater of them that we find we have assented before we are aware of it. Then the absolute ending of it hits us. His beloved body, lying so tenderly, grandly among us in the room, will be taken. The final dark intensity of him, the force of his presence, will be gone, given up. We gather around, touching his body one last time, the temperature now alien. We turn away and they work quickly, lifting him on to the stretcher, gently enfolding his body in cloth.

"We don't want to upset you but want you to know we will put straps around him so that as we round the corner and descend the short steps, we know he will not fall," the man says. His infinite and precise care in preparing us makes everything right. We nod and watch as they strap him in. Now he is an object wrapped in cloth.

They exit into the dark, some of the men following. Bob comes back in saying, "There's someone out there .... I know it's Dugan." Someone called him, of course. Bob sensed his athletic form pacing in the shadows. I should have called out for him to come in, but in the intensity of the moment, in my not having seen him for years, and in my having little comprehension of the falling out that had occurred between him and some of the others—I did not. Dugan drove an hour from his home and roamed outside for a least 4 hours, I learned later, until the man and woman from Pacific Interment came to take Mansfield away. He appeared alone down at their van just before they pulled away, the last person to touch him and bless him on his journey away from us.

People slowly begin to leave. When the last stragglers are gone, despite my automatic protestations that I am fine, I experience a sudden jolt of fear at being there alone, as if a dark wind can now just whistle through the place unobstructed. I feel a barking emptiness and have no protection, am now as open and vulnerable as a child. I notice for the first time a light on in the apartment we looked out on across the way. I marvel that I've never seen anyone there the entire time I've been here, in all the times I've been up in the middle of the night, but this one night ... as though some dark empty place has been waiting this whole time and now has light.

Before I open my pallet to sleep, I find on Mansfield's desk this poem on his Little Zen Calendar for this full moon Monday 7 May 2001.

> Bright bright!
> bright bright bright!
> bright bright!
> bright bright bright!
> bright bright, the moon!
> —Myoe

How he would love that, I think, and cherish it as though it has been written, not 800 years ago, but just now, for him.

Emptiness

May 8, 2001

I awaken and find the mattress a barren empty wreck in the middle of the front room. I open the curtains as usual. I must finally have allowed myself to sleep. When I look across the street, I see that not only is my brother gone, but my man from the construction site is gone too. This is the man my brother and I fantasized about being a good man, salt of the earth, with a loving wife at home, and though white-haired, lusty as a barnyard cock and my secret lover. I feel doubly desolate. My brother is gone and the fantasy we shared is gone. Moments later, I look over and see him standing nearby. His truck, for the first time since I've been here, is parked sideways and I did not recognize it. I feel absurdly relieved, as though if I can still inhabit the silly game Mansfield and I concocted together, somehow that means my brother is still with me.

I cannot bear that there is no conversation, no other. After being side-by-side with Mansfield around the clock for months, it feels impossible. I simply cannot tolerate it. I cannot sit still. I cannot work. The time for my regular exercise class approaches. I have not called to cancel it. I numbly think, why stay here when there is no reason for my being here anymore? Why do anything? I go. Pulling into the familiar tight parking lot, everything is different, as if all the world is unhinged from itself, all moorings loosed. Everything feels both too close and as if the canopy of the sky is now lifted to an infinite expansion. I walk the familiar cement corridor, registering the difference between last time I was here and this. There is a nothingness between those times so

vast I can only have hints of the dimension. I go about
the regular exercises, but there is a whole other exercise
taking place as my mind tries to take in the absence by
racing again and again over the familiar things that are
now gone. I lie on my back doing the leg lifts and exten-
sions that strengthen the abdominal muscles and my
eyes pool with tears. I allow it, and Carol says, "What's
up?" Since she's asked, I say, "My brother died last
night."

"Oh, my dear, why are you even here this morning?!"
she cries in her concern.

I start to say, "Why stay home?" then just give up. "I
don't know," I say. "I guess I'm not good for much of
anything today." I've been a provisional member of
Bodies Mind, registering month by month, never knowing how long I will be there, feeling somehow incapable
of initiating friendships, since telling the reason for my
being there felt as if it would burden others. Now I feel
almost ashamed of my aloneness. I throw on my long
shirt and, after thanking her for her caring and her good
sense, wander back out into the bright sun, where everything is strange and empty. I drive back through town.
Where I used to get coffee I wonder, why would I get
coffee? Where I shopped, I wonder, what for?

I return home, there being no reason to do anything.
The telephone keeps ringing. Names I've only heard
before or seen on Mansfield's list of far-flung friends
are now voices who want to connect, express their sense
of loss, tell their sweetest memories. More than one
person says to me, "He was my best friend." Or, "Of all
the people I knew then, it is your brother I have stayed
in touch with." He was the hub of a huge wheel of people spread around the world.

I talk at length with Zen Guy, much longer than on
the evening I met him. His presence over the phone is so
comforting; he is just there. He is telling me about the

seven days that the soul spends in the bardo, according to the Tibetan Book of the Dead, that there is this time before final departure. I am struck because, months before I arrived, while on the phone with Mansfield, the date May 14 came to me out of the blue as the day he would die. And he died on May 7th. The phone keeps beeping as Zen Guy and I talk, signalling a stream of other callers trying to get through. Because so many people want to connect and want news, I feel I must interrupt our conversation and answer the calls, just as Mansfield used to do when I talked with him from Boston. It feels like a bombardment, like arrows coming in in quick succession from around the country. My conversation with Zen Guy becomes thinner and thinner, a precious thread slipping through my fingers. It feels as though we are in an assembling crowd and are forced farther and farther apart until we are just two arms waving at each other. Finally, I give up and apologize, telling him I have to attend to everyone's questions. I feel a loss, like my access to a reflective pool has been taken away.

Dr. Pond calls. I am thanking him for all he did for Mansfield, when he pauses, then simply says, "It was so ... meaningful."

※ ※ ※

I go out to run an errand. The long stretch of Miller Ave. into town is listless and empty. What was lush, tree-lined, and charming now feels flat and endless, unrecognizable. A pang of fear flashes in me that I am somehow inexplicably lost in this alien landscape that should be familiar. When I return home, I realize that the message on Mansfield's answering machine is, of course, still his voice. People say they are haunted hearing the usual energy and command of his voice from before he was sick, as if nothing was different—a rude shock that increases their sorrow. Finally, Paul claims it. He wants to use it in an audio collage he will make as a loving musical tribute to his friend.

Elyse calls from Mexico. She cannot stop crying. Grief washes through her like a flash flood, a torrent of all the pain and sorrow and love she has been carrying these long years of his illness. And that she is away only amplifies her anguish—there is nothing she can do, nothing she can take care of for him, no service she can render. When she quiets, she tells a story. She was walking with a group up a trail into the spare countryside. She found herself walking alone—the others had moved on far ahead of her. A large crow alighted on the path directly in front of her. Standing facing her, it blocked her path, not allowing her to pass. There was this moment of intense encounter. Then it moved to fly away, and she was able to continue on up the path. Later she realized that moment occurred at the time of Mansfield's death. Listening to her, I see the singularity of that event and know that that would be my brother—dark black, shiny, intense, playful, a trickster, laughing his raucous laugh. I cry too, at the intensity of their love and the loss that has to be borne.

Condolences

May 10, 2001

Someone at work in Boston finds an email from Jack with the obituary he has lovingly written for Mansfield. The word is out in my universe there, and I realize I will now have to contend with another onslaught of phone calls and emails that a part of me wishes to hide from. It feels like an assault, the need to suddenly be public with something I have barely begun to calculate on the inside. I feel violated, a rage at everyone despite knowing people are well meaning and genuinely solicitous. Under the circumstances, condolences feel platitudinous, impoverished. My private inner reality has to be held separate. Maybe that is the whole point of the culturally orchestrated pageantry—to ease one into living with the loss ... to defer the full dull brunt and endless subtlety of its enormity and finality.

Dugan

June 6, 2001

Finally, I start to emerge from my stunned wandering to realize that there is a next thing, something I need to do. I start a slow, deliberative cleaning out of all Mansfield's possessions. It proves a sweet, meditative labor. I find three identical pairs of white jeans I recalled Mansfield automatically and optimistically buying on an early excursion we had taken with Emma to Marin City. I marvel at his orderly and redundant supplies, like an artist's materials laid side-by-side, ready so no intervening thought nor extraneous action is needed. Stashed in his big oak desk I find lists of words and phrases written on all sizes of note pads in his bright roller-ball inks or fine magic marker. Did he hear them, read them, think of them? He certainly collected them. I find a short recording of him reading something of his, and he intones with the hallowed solemnity of an old poet.

In the midst of the disarray, I call Dugan. I came across a cache of my brother's favorite talismans: a tiny metal lingam from Thailand to be worn around the neck on a leather thong, a disc with a bas relief of a Hindu deity, a thicket of tiny skulls. I met Dugan and his family on two or three occasions over the years. We make a date to take a walk in the woods off Tennessee Valley Road. It is a late afternoon, after his work. The woods are dense and lush from the long winter rains, a place where they are reclaiming the indigenous trees, encouraging them to grow in place of the ubiquitous eucalyptus. We walk until we come to a small clearing where a bridge passes over the stream.

"You know, I was only 14 when I met your brother," Dugan says. "So, I've known him most of my life. I learned so much from him. He actually taught me how to think." In his restless physicality, Dugan jumps up on top of the bridge handrail and balances there, four feet off the ground, pelting pebbles into the water. "I really learned about life from him," he says. "I loved him. Revered him, really." Eventually, we both sit on the railing.

"He told me that when he got his diagnosis, you said you would see him every day. He was blown away by that," I say.

"Yah," says Dugan, "I would have too."

"You know, when you had your falling out from the group or whatever that was, I think the only thing he could manage was to cut you out," I say. "You know how implacable he could be, how black and white. He was paring down to the essentials and couldn't deal with the slightest controversy. Some close friends of mine really wanted to meet him and I had to say no, because he told me it was all he could do to muster the energy to be in short conversations with the people he loved." I want to comfort Dugan, whose loss just now feels greater than my own.

"I know he loved you and Sherry and the kids completely," I say. "He told me the stories about your twilight hikes out the Tennessee Valley path to the ocean—the time you guys encountered that mountain lion."

"Yah ... that was something .... It was hard for Dylan and Desmond to understand why suddenly they couldn't see him anymore. I have to remember our relationship as it was." He says this as though this is the lifeline that will help him get his bearings on how to continue living without his beloved friend. I see for a moment the 14-year-old boy—wild, unruly, an outlaw. He is still that boy, but heavier, handsomer, with the same physicality busting out of him.

As if satisfied, he says, "It helps so much to talk about him. I could talk about him forever."

"Let's go find you some stuff," I say.

We jump down from the railing and head back along the path, swapping stories the whole way. Back at the apartment, we tear into everything. He takes artwork, kitchen things ("I remember this!"), a wall hanging, and, finally, clothes, as if he can bring the body back by wearing them, a feeling I've had, myself.

"Anything but the worn suede jacket," I say, "That belongs to Elyse."

Emma graduates

June 8, 2001

I sit at dinner in Chicago, the night before Emma's graduation, with Jay's and Emma's families. Jay and Emma have been a couple for most of her time at the University of Chicago. Jay's lusty and noisy uncle George, who would endear himself to me forever by casually handing me a small chocolate chip cookie at the ceremony the next day, sits at the far end of the table surrounded by his beautiful daughters. Jay's mother Margaret is across from me, vibrant, alert. Susan's aging mother, Jeanie, all 91 years of her, entirely fay, sits beside me with her wispy halo of white hair, telling sweet stories interlaced with ribald editorial comments delivered in a loud sotto voce, making it unclear whether she is deaf or just loves being hilariously outrageous and rude. Susan, her boyfriend Tom and her demanding sister Nancy, both of whom I am meeting for the first time, are there. Jay's father Ted sits opposite me. He asks me a question. I think of Mansfield immediately and cannot keep back my tears. I feel immobilized—struck dumb by the intensity of my emotion, it's closeness to the surface, a month after his death. In some undefined way, I feel called upon to stand in for my brother, whom they have never met, to represent the other side of Emma's family. Yet I feel entirely incapable of doing so in my collapse. I am mad that Mansfield did not get to witness this graduation, with honors, of his cherished daughter from a great and challenging school. I am mad that her achievement, which would so have pleased him, is tempered by his death only 33 days ago. I am mad that three and a half years of her undergraduate life were informed by the ever-present weight of sadness. The next day, after the graduation ceremony, we stroll through the warm spring Chicago neighborhood, walking behind Emma and Jay, who are hand in hand and exuding the sweetness of their youth, beauty and promise.

Procession

June 24, 2001

A large group gathers at the horse farm parking lot at Tennessee Valley. We make a long, motley assembly in slow procession along Mansfield's favorite walk to the ocean ... Emma, Elyse, Fran and Bob, Paul and Teresa, Susan and Tom, Lightnin' and Tokey, Jonathan, Orit, John and Emily, Jean and many others I don't know. At the beach, the conclusion of our walk, I cannot bear the moment of tension when no one moves to take the ashes. I rush in to fill the emptiness. Since Mansfield has been at my side from the moment I was born, in some way I feel that he is mine. I dig into the ashes and run blindly to the edge of the water and throw them out into the suspending air. Of course, Elyse has a closer, deeper claim and certainly Emma the closest of all. They proceed slowly, with dignity, awareness, reverence. I see that, in the agitated intensity of my own emotions, I may have acted in a way that hurt or insulted others. But in the solemnity of the moment, each person's inner relationship with Mansfield is given expression in ritual. Tolerance is conferred.

Despite the recent history, Dugan's love will not be denied. Though he is not in the procession, he has created his own shrine to Mansfield, a long cleft in the rock protected from the wind, where he has collected stones, wildflowers, grasses and items that bespeak their years of friendship. The last thirteen of which included walks along this trail, talks on this beach.

Eight years later

August, 2009

In 2009, eight years after Mansfield's death, Fran and I
returned to Boston from Cape Cod, where we were
visiting her husband Bob's family. Back in town, it was a
gruelingly hot summer day—97 degrees with a saturating
humidity and wavers of heat issuing up from the sticky
blacktop. Fran and I drove straight to the Shepard
Fairey exhibit at the Institute for Contemporary Art, the
mercifully spacious and cool modern structure on the
waterfront. We took the elevator to the top floor and
watched a short film on Fairey, the street artist. Fran
said that he now inhabited her old studio in LA. In a
shot of the studio, she pointed to where she had hung
her 20-year-old nude self-portrait above the entrance on
Sunset Boulevard, those many years ago.

We moved out into the cavernous rooms, two of just
a few people at the exhibit. The sheer size of Fairey's
work dominated the viewer viscerally, producing an awe
I experienced as slightly uncomfortable. I walked up to a
huge piece and was studying the technique of it from a
few inches away: a kind of palimpsest made of old newspaper text and cartoons, fine red handwriting and a pale
wash of the same color that made the whole seem as if it
was emerging into focus through time. I remarked with
admiration on the finely cut stencils that were, surprisingly, still embedded there too. Fran, standing in front
of a large Fairey painting across the way, observed casually, "You know, Mansfield had a mean Exacto knife."

In that moment, as I examined the intricacies of the
cutwork in front of me, I saw my brother bending over
his own work, absorbed in the infinitely exacting craft of

it, lost to time in his perfecting—the same joy and discovery there as when he found the cache of drawings in the old Colt house attic, decades before. And in my mind, I heard his daughter Emma's voice over the telephone from a conversation we'd had just a few days before. She had exclaimed, "I love surgery!" expressing surprise and delight at the potency of this passion that had lain fallow until she happened upon it in her latest medical school rotation. I saw that Mansfield's lovingly honed mastery with an Exacto knife, refined through Fran's tutelage, fine-tuned in that LA studio, was alive again in the thrill of discovery in Emma's voice, in her enthusiasm for using a scalpel skillfully. The recognition of it was ecstatic: it was as if I could hear his high laugh relishing the absurd simplicity and obviousness of it all. As though he himself were right there with us, now fully satisfied.

EPILOGUE

Mansfield answered the phone always with the single word, "YES!" as though everything coming his way was to be affirmed. He had a magic he couldn't see. I have learned now to pay attention to how he lives in me. Isn't love the deepest mirror? Having watched him, I know that we shine despite ourselves, in ways we don't even know—that he struggled so with his sense of place and legacy and couldn't even see the trail of light he left behind.

Acknowledgments

I began writing this book in the spring of 2002 when I found early encouragement from Mansfield's extended San Francisco family, as well as Cliff Hakim, Mary Jacobsen, Scott Campbell, Jack Mueller, Nina Kruschwitz and Bill Torbert. Amory Wallace observed that it could be much longer than the original two pages I produced. Christine Harris and Vicky Schubert were patient readers of early efforts. I was lucky to be invited into a writing group hosted by former Houghton Mifflin editor, Lawrence Kessenich, which became a much-valued source of practice, feedback and support. The description of Mansfield's artistic development is borrowed liberally from the obituary Jack Mueller so lovingly wrote about him; specifics were verified with Fran Valesco.

Lawrence Kessenich served as an invaluable editor at two critical points in the book's development; Cat Parnell's editorial prowess supplied essential discipline and perspective. Thanks also go to Bob Eiland, Amy Ellsworth, Renee Caso, Tina Silander Clark, Michael Eramo, Joanne Yawitz, Heather Ahrenholz, Eileen Christelow, Robin Otto, Susann Cook-Greuter, Grady McGonagill, David Perkins and Karen Kita who provided generous feedback. My former writer's group, Mary Bonina and Margery Gans shared their considerable experience and discerning encouragement.

Anne Starr

Anne Starr's "Evening" was nominated for *Best Microfiction 2023 Anthology*. She holds an MBA from Simmons College. She spent her childhood in Michigan, Vermont and Ontario, and now lives in Cambridge, Massachusetts.